★★★★★★★★★★★★★★ A ★★★★★★★★★★★★★★
GIANT
REBORN

ALSO BY JOHAN VAN OVERTVELDT

The Chicago School

Bernanke's Test

The End of the Euro

A GIANT REBORN

Why the US Will Dominate the 21st Century

Johan Van Overveldt

AN AGATE IMPRINT

CHICAGO

Printed in the United States

Library of Congress Cataloging-in-Publication Data

Overtveldt, Johan van.
 A giant reborn : why the US will dominate the 21st century / Johan Van Overtveldt.
    pages cm
  Summary: ""An analysis of global economic affairs, making the case that the United States will continue to be the world's sole superpower in the 21st century"--Provided by publisher"-- Provided by publisher.
 Includes bibliographical references and index.
 ISBN 978-1-932841-81-7 (hardback) -- ISBN 1-932841-81-4 (hard cover)
 1. United States--Economic policy--21st century. 2. United States--Politics and government--21st century. 3. United States--Foreign relations--21st century. I. Title.
 HC106.84.O94 2015
 327.73001'12--dc23
                        2015013356

10 9 8 7 6 5 4 3 2 1   15 14 13 12 11

B2 Books is an imprint of Agate Publishing.

Agate books are available in bulk at discount prices. For more information, go to agatepublishing.com.

Dedicated to the memory of Milton Friedman and Gary Becker.
Superb scholars, generous men.

Contents

Introduction

Decline, Once More

Wags have long credited Otto von Bismarck (1818–1898), the legendary Prussian aristocrat and statesman known as the founding father of modern Germany, with saying that "a special Providence" protects "children, drunkards and the United States of America." Perhaps in his day, that was true, but lately, that Providence that Bismarck supposedly referenced seems to have finally given up on the United States. In high-level discussions since the late 2000s, the United States is generally cast not as a dominant force in world affairs, but instead as being in unstoppable decline. Chestnuts like *America, the hyper-power* or the *one-dimensional American world order* are no longer commonly heard. *The American Century*, it seems, is over, and it's time for something new.

Details of the story, as well as how fast the fall from glory will be, vary from one messenger to the next, but the conclusion is the same: America is in decline. "An empire enthralled with its own power and unaware that it is fading," so the *New York Times* described the United States in 2007.[1] Whether the topic is hard or soft power, or both, the United States is perceived as rapidly losing its place at the top. Alfred McCoy, a professor of history at the University of Wisconsin–Madison, declared in 2010 that

> the demise of the United States as the global superpow-er could come far more quickly than anyone imagines. If Washington is dreaming of 2040 or 2050 as the end of the American Century, a more realistic assessment of domestic and global trends suggests that in 2025, just 15 years from now, it could all be over except for the shouting.[2]

Early in 2014 Peter Beinart, a professor at City University of New York and former editor of *The New Republic*, wrote an article entitled "The End of American Exceptionalism."[3] Michael Snyder of The American Dream blog echoed the same theme:

> The reality is that the United States is in a deep state of decline, and it is getting harder to deny that fact with each passing day. Mentally, emotionally, physically, spiritually and financially we are a train wreck.... We have abandoned the values and the principles that early Americans held so dear, and as a result our society is a giant mess.[4]

Snyder goes on to list 55 items illustrating his argument for America's "deep state of decline."[5]

Empires and superpowers come and go with regularity. The United States has followed in the footsteps of the British Empire, the hegemonic world power from the end of the Napoleonic Wars in 1815 to the start of World War I in 1914. It's safe to say that

> global history from 1500 to 1945 is a lengthy treatise of increasing contact and conflict among a series of great regional powers. Some of these powers achieved supra-regional empires, with the Spanish, French and English being the most obvious. Several regional pow-

ers—Austria, German Ottoman Turkey and Japan—
also succeeded in extending their writ over huge tracts
of territory during parts of this period. And several sec-
ondary powers—the Netherlands, Poland, China and
Portugal—had periods of relative strength. Yet the two
world wars massively devastated all of these powers.[6]

It's worth mentioning that none of these historic powers
achieved the degree of dominance attained by the United States
in the years immediately following World War II. Not even Great
Britain came close.

Great Britain's dominance was largely due to its primacy in
the first Industrial Revolution and its naval forces. Notably, its demise was swift. In the words of legendary international investor
Jim Rogers: "After overseeing an empire on which the sun never
set, the country descended into economic chaos within a single
generation and was bankrupt within three."[7] During the inter-
war period, the United States took over as the leading nation in
the world, but the Roaring Twenties were quickly followed by the
Great Depression, which hit the United States harder than practically any other country in the world. In the wake of World War II,
however, the United States rose again to world prominence.

In 1941, *Time* and *Life* publisher Henry Luce first advanced
the concept of the twentieth century as

> the first great American Century [with] America as the
> dynamic center ever-widening spheres of enterprise,
> America as the training center of the skillful servants of
> mankind, America as the Good Samaritan, really believ-
> ing again that it is more blessed to give than to receive,
> and America as powerhouse of the ideals of Freedom
> and Justice.[8]

Of course, America's ascendance to absolute world power was greatly helped by the fact that two world wars had simply "cleared away the competition."[9]

When the communist Soviet Union, America's only real challenger during that period, collapsed at the end of the 1980s, the world seemed to have become unipolar. The United States had won the Cold War. According to some analysts, the end of history had arrived: Liberal democracy, as embodied in the ideology and values defended by the United States, was well on its way to conquering the world.[10] In this context, US President George H.W. Bush addressed Congress in early 1991, in the aftermath of the first Gulf War. Bush spoke of a "new world order" in which "freedom and respect for human rights find a home among all nations," and concluded that "the Gulf War put this new world order to its first test and, my fellow Americans, we passed that test."[11]

Almost a quarter century later, not much remains of the victorious mood that followed the end of the Cold War. Even worse, so the declinist dogma goes, a *rapid* decline of the United States as a superpower is now unavoidable.[12] If the American Century began in 1945, then, the Century will be considerably less than 100 years. American declinism theory basically consists of two tracks: one internal, the other external.

Internal factors bringing about America's supposed decline are related to successive, accumulating policy failures. Global economist David Malpass stated: "Though a great nation, we are making such deep policy mistakes that we are in decline."[13] The list of events is long and includes the events of 9/11, which proved how vulnerable the homeland had become; the unsuccessful and costly wars in Iraq and Afghanistan; the enormous damage done to the US government's moral posture due to the mistreatment of prisoners at Guantanamo Bay and Abu Ghraib; the US's difficulty in dealing with a nuclear Iran; the massive financial crisis of 2008–2009, which was followed by the worst recession since the Great Depression; escalating government debt; the ever more rising costs of Social Security and Medicare; the disastrous start of Obamacare; revelations of outrageous overstepping of boundaries by the National Security Agency; and tepid responses to the crises in Syria and Ukraine and to the gruesome threats of the Islamic State…just to name a few. These perceived policy failures give fuel to those who believe Washington, DC is as decadent and impotent as Rome during the fall of its first empire.[14]

Declinists believe that this internal degradation is not reserved for the political, economic, and military spheres; they find it is even more pervasive in the cultural and personal spheres. W. James Antle III, associate editor of *The American Spectator*, has groused that America's

> culture is awash in the raw sewage of vulgarity and ava-
> rice. The family is shattered. The average American can-
> not articulate why marriage is not a unisex institution.
> One baby out of three is born out of wedlock. Another
> million per year are snuffed out in the womb. We are
> bound by no common faith or culture. Mass immigra-
> tion, much of it illegal, without accompanying assimila-
> tion may deprive us of a common language.[15]

Serial entrepreneur Jim Manzi attributes this internal degrada-
tion to problems of inequality and poor educational achievement among some Americans, and relates these issues to dysfunctional American families. Manzi argues:

> The level of family disruption in America is enormous
> compared to almost every other country in the world. Of
> course, out-of-wedlock births are as common in many
> European countries as they are in the United States. But
> the estimated percentage of 15-year-olds living with
> both of their biological parents is far lower in the Unit-
> ed States than in Western Europe, because unmarried

European partners are much more likely to raise children together. It is hard to exaggerate the chaotic conditions under which something like a third of American children are being raised—or to overstate the negative impact this disorder has on their academic achievement, social skills, and character formation. There are certainly heroic exceptions, but the sad fact is that most of these children could not possibly compete with their foreign counterparts.... The social capital transmitted by intact families has therefore become a more and more relevant source of competitive advantage.[16]

External factors attributed to leading America's decline include China's rise, most significantly, but also the strides taken by India, Brazil, Russia, and the European Union (EU). With a population of 1.3 billion and an economy capable of virtually unlimited growth, China is quickly catching up with the United States, economically speaking. During the past quarter century, China has turned around its backward, horrendously inefficient economic system, transforming itself into the preeminent industrial factory of the world. More recently, the country has begun to specialize in technology. Its military capabilities have grown in line with its economic expansion, with a focus on countering America's naval dominance of the Pacific.[17] Its huge international financial reserves offer ample opportunities for foreign investment and strengthen China's political leverage around the world.

China's political system remains essentially dictatorial, with the People's Communist Party as the sole accepted political power in the country. Of course, this can be seen as much more efficient than the US's democratic system, which is plagued by stalemate and pointless infighting and is unable to deal effectively with the challenges confronting American society. Some believe that the United States is falling behind as a consequence of mediocre or outright poor internal decision making, while China marches on and will shortly become the dominating force in the world.

Not everyone, however, is on board with the declinists' storyline. During his 2012 State of the Union address, President Barack Obama declared that "anyone who tells you that America is in decline or that our influence has waned, doesn't know what they're talking about." Of course, it's not surprising to hear positive rhetoric from the president, but what about the words of Lee Kuan Yew, founding prime minister and longtime leader of Singapore, who argued, "America will not be reduced to second-rate status. Historically, the United States has demonstrated a great capacity for renewal and revival"?[18] Strategic planning consultant Tsvi Bisk claimed, "The 21st century promises to be the American Century to an even greater extent than the 20th."[19] *Wall Street Journal* columnist William McGurn provided his own "short answer" to the question *is America in decline?* "Of course not."[20] German political analyst Josef Joffe, author of the 2014 book *The Myth of America's Decline,* wrote of "a half century of false prophecies" on the fall of the United States as the dominant world power.[21] Others are cautiously optimistic, like *Financial Times* reporter Geoff Dyer: "If the United States can clean its own financial house and avoid the temptations of either confrontation or isolation, it will still hold many of the best cards in the twenty-first century."[22]

Despite these arguments and indications of a slow turnaround in the worldwide perspective on the United States, an optimistic view of its future as the principal force in world affairs is in the minority. As a longtime observer from a European perspective of the United States and of world developments in general, I share this minority view. As others busy themselves performing burial rites for the United States, I present the prospect of *A Giant Reborn*—specifically, *A Giant Reborn, Once More.* Decline and rebirth do indeed seem to have been its defining characteristic from the very beginning.

This book, you will find, is organized into four chapters. The first regards US declinism, a view on the country's evolution that's even older than the country itself.

The second chapter describes a process I call *turbochange*, fired by the earthly trinity of growth in knowledge and human capital, entrepreneurship, and globalization. This earthly trinity, I believe, will lead not just to change but to intense change, thus justifying the "turbo" prefix. Turbochange is very demanding on a society's structure, and powerful forces will likely develop to counter and even block it.

In the third chapter, I explore my belief that American society is ideally equipped to take advantage of turbochange.

In the fourth chapter, I contrast these characteristics of American society with those of China and EU nations, as they remain the strongest international competition. The epilogue places a remarkable recent event—the so-called shale revolution—in the context of the insights developed in the earlier chapters.

Chapter 1

Downbound from the Start

After defeating the British Empire in a brutal war for independence, the young republic was soundly swatted back into its place less than 30 years later during the War of 1812. The war saw US forces routed in Canada, US sailors captured and impressed into duty on British warships, US ports blockaded, and the US Capitol and White House set ablaze by a British invasion force. When measured against its own position just a generation earlier—it appeared that the United States had declined drastically.[23]

THIS PORTRAYAL OF THE FIRST DECADES OF AMERICA'S young life doesn't depict a great start. Such a description belies the country's rapid rise in the 20th century. Former Treasury secretary and Harvard economics professor Larry Summers wrote, "American history has been...a history of alarm and concern.... Predictions of America's decline are as old as the republic."[24] As a matter of fact, one can find declinist predictions as far back as the very birth of the independent republic.

Cotton Mather, a stern Puritan minister, often thundered against the cheating and lying taking place in Massachusetts Bay

Colony decades before American independence. He claimed these vices would inevitably bring the territory and its people down. According to Josef Joffe, Mather "deserves the title of First American Declinist."[25]

The mainstream European view in those days was that "due chiefly to atmospheric conditions, in particular excessive humidity, all living things in the Americas were not only inferior to those found in Europe but also in a condition of decline."[26] German philosopher Immanuel Kant concluded in 1775 that Americans should be considered "a not yet properly formed (or half degenerated) subrace…too weak for hard work, too indifferent to pursue anything carefully, incapable of all culture, in fact even lower than the Negro."[27] Thomas Moore, an Irish poet who traveled throughout America in the early 19th century, echoed Kant's sentiments.[28] The great Charles Darwin saw no future for Americans and their country.[29] Talk of decline and failure was even commonplace in correspondence between Thomas Jefferson and John Adams, two of America's founding fathers.

In the 1870s, however, French lawyer Simon Linguet warned that adventurers populating the North American continent would easily turn the enormous resources available there into a formidable economic power. Linguet even warned that Europe was likely to be invaded and destroyed by the Americans.[30]

Talk of declinism seemed genetically encoded in America's nature. British novelist Charles Dickens noted that "if its individual citizens, to a man, are to be believed, [the United States] always is depressed, and always is stagnated, and always is at an alarming crisis, and never was otherwise."[31]

This gloom probably had a lot to do with the fact that the United States was a country looking for an identity. The war against the British had been a coordinated revolt among separate colonies. The colonies were forced to cooperate; otherwise, the British could not be defeated. To prevent tyranny within their own new government, the Founding Fathers created an alliance that transferred most of the power to the states. The federal government was intentionally left weak, despite the enormous expansion of the territory via the 1803 Louisiana Purchase from France and the accession of Texas in 1845. This soul-searching of a nation led directly to the Civil War of 1861–65.[32]

Roller Coaster Ride

The Civil War was the bloody culmination of tensions between the North and South that had been building since the earliest days of the republic. There is substantial evidence that the Founding Fathers were fully aware of this problem, believing that the tensions were temporarily, at best, put to rest when the nation was founded. While the Constitution was still being written, James Madison observed: "It seems now to be pretty well understood that the real difference of interests lies not between the large and small but between the Northern and Southern states. The institution of slavery and its consequences form the line."[33] The South's domination of national politics from 1789 on hardly helped resolve the issue.

The Civil War brought hitherto unseen episodes of savagery, murder, brutality, decay, death, and destruction to the United States. Close to 4 million people died during the war, more than the total number of American casualties in the two world wars of the 20th century. This is all the more surprising given that the outcome was never really in doubt, given the enormous industrial and demographic imbalance between North and South.[34]

Although it is often argued that slavery was the primary issue of the Civil War, the conflict was fundamentally about preservation of the Union. "After Lincoln's murder," so Alan Dowd argued,

> General Sherman openly feared America's slipping into anarchy. The Union general wondered "who was left on this continent to give order and shape to the now

disjointed elements of the government." The war had rolled back American civilization, and recovery of what was lost was anything but certain. America had declined immeasurably—or perhaps better said, descended.[35]

Although the Civil War left deep scars on the American soul, this period of decline eventually reversed, and the long-sought unity was finally achieved: "The bloody Civil War affirmed a new sense of nationhood and resolved some long-standing debates; slavery was unacceptable in the land of liberty, so too was the idea of secession."[36] Only after the Civil War, argued Thomas McCraw, a Harvard Business School professor of business history, "did people speak of the nation in the singular: 'the United States *is*' rather than 'the United States *are*.' [37]

The Civil War and years that followed it perfectly illustrated the Yew quote mentioned in the introduction, about America's "capacity for renewal and revival." Beyond reversing the nation's decline, the end of the Civil War revitalized the country. The controversial Abraham Lincoln was martyred and became "transmuted into the icon of the reborn nation."[38]

A critical piece of this successful rebirth was Lincoln's policy of quickly reintegrating the rebellious South into the fold of the Union, without seeking revenge. After Lincoln's assassination, his successor, Andrew Johnson, pushed Lincoln's policy through, despite considerable congressional opposition.

The world took notice. The French journalist and intellectual Michel Chevalier noted immediately after the end of the Civil War that the United States was destined to become a great power. He urged European nations to pull together, given the "political colossus that has been created at the other side of the Atlantic."[39]

The evolution of the United States during this period can be best characterized as following a roller-coaster pattern, with decay and chaos alternating with rebirth and progress. The Civil War came very close to destroying the Union. When it was over, the United States was whole again and, perhaps more importantly, had sobered up. The young nation was "flushed with self-confidence, intoxicated with the exuberance of its own freedom," British lawyer and diplomat James Bryce concluded, and had "purged away these faults of youth and inexperience…the stern discipline of the Civil War taught it sobriety, and in giving it something to be really proud of, cleared away the fumes of self-conceit."[40]

At the same time, "the transcontinental railroad and the telegraph turned the United States into a single, vast market that drove rapid industrialization and attracted immigrants by the tens of millions."[41] Big business moved to the center of American industrial and economic progress.

The post–Civil War era was also the scene for the rise of the so-called robber barons, such as John D. Rockefeller, Andrew Carnegie, J.P. Morgan, and Cornelius Vanderbilt. These energetic men helped shape the country by dominating the Industrial Revolution, albeit in an often ruthless, and sometimes even criminal, way.[42]

So, a period of great optimism ensued in the United States as a result of the end of the Civil War and in Europe as a result of the end of the Franco–Prussian War (1870–71). But all good things must come to an end. Less than a decade after the end of the Civil War, the gloom returned.

Starting in Austria in May 1873, a financial panic began as speculation-driven excesses sent prices of financial assets through the roof. That September, the panic spread to the United States, focused first on the Northern Pacific Railway.[43] Afterward, a contraction in economic activity known as the "Long Depression" began, lasting from October 1873 through March 1879. This 65-month-long recession still stands as the longest in American history—even longer than the Great Depression. Close to 20,000 businesses and ten states went bankrupt, and the unemployment rate peaked at 14 percent. Although growth intensified after 1879, deflation stubbornly continued, and several new recessions took place before the end of the century. In 1884, a new financial panic slammed America.

During the last two decades of the 19th century, American presidents and their administrations found that they had little control over the financial and economic turmoil that hit the country and its citizens. The troubles were so pervasive that these presidents came to be known as the "No Name Presidents."

"No Fears for the Future"

After a 1909 trip to the United States, Sigmund Freud, the founding father of psychoanalysis, had described the country as "a mistake, a gigantic mistake,"[44] but his opinion was in the minority. Around the same time, British journalist W.T. Stead defined "Americanization of the world" as "the trend of the twentieth century." Stead wrote that "the advent of the United States of America as the greatest of world-Powers is the greatest political, social, and commercial phenomenon of our times."[45]

The United States had indeed recovered from the consequences of the Civil War and the Long Depression, in large part due to the expansion and improvement of the nation's transportation and communications networks. It was also exercising its economic and military muscles abroad. By the end of the 19th century, the country had become an important colonial power, mostly as a consequence of its quick and decisive victory in the Spanish–American War of 1898. In 1898 and 1899, the United States annexed Puerto Rico, the Philippines, Guam, the Hawaiian islands, and the port of Samoa." Cuba remained independent, but mostly in name; the US Army dominated the island. "In an 18-month period [the United States] had become the master of empires in the Caribbean and the Pacific," Daniel Bell concluded.[46]

Theodore Roosevelt played a very important role in "the advent of the United States of America as the greatest of world-Powers."[47]

Roosevelt became president of the United States following William McKinley's assassination in September 1901. Roosevelt had been the leader of the Navy Department of the US Army since 1897, creating what came to be known as the Great White Fleet. During his presidency, which lasted through 1909, Roosevelt vigorously fought business monopolies, lowered taxes, took decisive steps to increase food safety, and protected the natural treasures of the country.

Roosevelt was empowered by America's military successes toward the end of the 19th century; his motto regarding international affairs was "speak softly and carry a big stick." His policies led to construction of the Panama Canal, and he was an early proponent of America's entry into World War I. Moreover, Roosevelt became the first American president to emphasize the critical role of Asia in American power, stating: "The commerce and command of the Pacific will be factors of incalculable moment in the world's history."[48]

Talk of the demise of America reemerged after World War I, when the United States initially declined to step into the power vacuum left by the crumbling British Empire. Against the wishes of then-president Woodrow Wilson, Congress rejected the concept of the League of Nations in 1919, convincing the rest of the world that the United States was not ready (or perhaps not capable) to take the lead in world affairs.

But again, during the 1920s, declinism melted like snow in the sun. American companies widely commercialized a series of new technologies: machinery, automobiles, chemical products, radio, film, photography, and much more. Henry Ford's Model T started the worldwide automobile revolution that fundamentally changed the world economy and the lives of millions. By the end of the decade, Detroit was producing eight times as many automobiles as Britain, France, and Germany combined.[49] In 1924, Russian leader Josef Stalin told party workers that "the combination of Russian revolutionary sweep and American efficiency is the essence of Leninism."[50]

Of course, it didn't last. The Roaring Twenties rolled right into the Great Depression of the 1930s. For most Americans and the world at large, this unhappy turnaround came as a complete surprise. On the occasion of his inauguration as next president of the United States, Herbert Hoover declared on March 4, 1929: "We have reached a higher degree of comfort and security than ever existed before in the history of the world.... I have no fears for the future of our country. It is bright with hope."[51]

A few months later, Wall Street crashed. A recession followed, but a series of policy mistakes turned it into the Great Depression. The mistakes came especially in the fields of international trade, banking, and monetary policy.[52] Unemployment and poverty escalated at breathtaking speed. Hoover's administration and Congress, it seemed, had no answers for this extreme economic and social crisis, and declinism returned with a vengeance. Not only did the Great Depression cripple American prosperity, it also undermined the self-confidence of the country and its citizens. So deep was the malaise and the desperation that a leading commentator argued, "What we have lost is, it may be, not merely our way in the economic labyrinth but our conviction of the value of what we are doing."[53]

Hoover was succeeded by Franklin Roosevelt, who immediately began rebuilding the confidence of the American nation and its people. On top of the huge social and economic problems the new president inherited, he also had to deal with the prospect of war. Despite continuous provocations by the Japanese and the Germans, the United States was initially unwilling to join World War II. Adolf Hitler concluded that America "was a weak country, incapable, because of its racial mixture and feeble democratic government, of organizing and maintaining strong military forces."[54] The German dictator told a friend, "What is America but millionaires, beauty queens, stupid records and Hollywood?... Transfer [a German] to Miami and you make a degenerate out of him—in other words—an American."[55]

The Japanese attack on Pearl Harbor on December 7, 1941, which killed 2,403 Americans and sank or damaged three cruisers, three destroyers, and eight battleships, made a deep impression on the American mind. Modern readers cannot help but see similarities to impressions of the 9/11 terrorist attacks in the following words regarding the Pearl Harbor attack:

> No American who lived through that Sunday will ever forget it. It seared deeply into the national consciousness, shearing away illusions that had been fostered for generations. And with the first shock came a sort of panic. This struck at our deepest pride. It tore at the myth of our invulnerability. Striking at the precious legend of our might, it seemed to leave us naked and defenseless.[56]

"We Will Bury You"

Immediately after the Allied victory in World War II, the United States seemed to be in an overwhelming position of strength. It dominated the Bretton Woods monetary management negotiations; as a result, postwar economic and financial order was organized around the US dollar. United States dominance was based on its economic power:

> The United States accounted for an absolute majority of all global manufacturing output, had the world's most technologically advanced economy with ample supplies of natural resources, and could protect this state of affairs with an essentially invincible military that possessed a nuclear monopoly. Most of the rest of the world was in ruins, pre-industrial, or under control of communist regimes that smothered economic initiative.[57]

President Harry Truman was as clear as he was brief when he declared: "We are the giant of the economic world."[58]

Shortly after the war, British socialist politician Harold Laski described the United States as the country that would soon "bestrode the world like a colossus; neither Rome at the height of its power nor Great Britain in the period of its economic supremacy enjoyed an influence so direct, so profound, or so pervasive."[59] The United States relied on its economic and military power to build a reservoir of international prestige and gratitude via its efforts to rebuild economies and societies crushed by war in Western Europe and Japan. The air bridge it organized in 1948 to keep Berlin supplied during a Russian siege "helped transform America from enemy to friend in the minds of millions of Germans."[60] The United States also supported colonies in Africa and Asia as they revolted against the European powers that dominated them.

But despite so many signs of strength and dominance, a sense of gloom began to permeate the American mind and soul. In March 1943, the American weekly *Life* favorably compared the Soviet Union to the United States and described Lenin as "perhaps the greatest man of modern times." The postwar division of Europe, the Soviet acquisition of nuclear weapons in 1949 (breaking up America's nuclear monopoly), the loss of China to the communists, the start of the Cold War, the stalemate in the Korean peninsula, and the Soviet invasion of Hungary all inspired talk of American decline.[61] Sounding much like Hitler years before, Soviet dictator Stalin openly joked about America's Korean adventure: "America's primary weapons…are stockings, cigarettes and other merchandise. They want to subjugate the world, yet they cannot subdue little Korea."[62] War hero Douglas MacArthur came into sharp conflict with US President Harry Truman regarding the Korean conflict,[63] elaborating during his keynote address to the Republican National Convention of 1952 on "our own relative decline."[64]

There was just as much trouble at home as there was abroad. Senator Joseph McCarthy, with the help of Richard Nixon, openly hunted for American communists inside the State Department and Hollywood during the first part of the 1950s. McCarthy's quest was truly paranoid and out of control, but it was based on a kernel of truth. "The problem," historian David Reynolds argued, "was that although McCarthy was indeed an unsavoury rabble-rouser, his sensationalized accusations were not completely unfounded— as the Truman administration knew well."[65]

McCarthyism was a dark chapter in the history of American civil liberties, sullying America's reputation and popularity around the world. In the early 1950s, the British scholar and commentator Denis Brogan warned of the "illusion of American omnipotence."[66] More than anything else, the Soviet Union would become the symbol of that lack of American omnipotence.

In November 1956, Soviet leader Nikita Khrushchev removed all doubt as to his stance on the topic of American decline, warning a group of Western ambassadors gathered at the Polish embassy in Moscow, "We will bury you." Less than a year later, the Soviets launched the Sputnik rocket into space, reinforcing the fear that the United States was losing the military and space race to the Soviets.[67]

Sputnik shock inspired US President Dwight Eisenhower to establish the National Aeronautics and Space Agency (NASA) and the Defense Advanced Research Projects Agency (DARPA). The Americans tried to catch up with the Soviets, rushing the Vanguard rocket into development. The Vanguard exploded on its first launch, at the end of 1957, and came to be known as Flopnik. The incident inspired Soviet delegates to make a cynical proposition: offering the United States aid from a Soviet fund for underdeveloped countries.[68]

Fear of the Soviet Union surpassing the United States as the leading nation of the world was so great in the late 1950s that Sam

Rayburn, then the Speaker of the House, thundered about the prospect of "Russian rubles [becoming] the coin of the land."[69] The fear behind these remarks: that the Sputnik triumph was just one example of the superior organization of the Soviet economy. State planning, many feared, was beating market economics. When in 1959 then–vice president Richard Nixon visited Moscow, Khrushchev did not mince words: "in another seven years, we'll be at the level of America, and after that we'll go farther. As we pass you by, we'll wave 'hi' to you, and then if you want, we'll stop and say, 'please come along behind us'."[70]

Only much later did observers learn that the Soviet Union's rapid growth was largely based on its ruthless transfer of people and resources from agriculture into industry. Such forced industrialization was not replicable in a more modern economy.

Cuba, Vietnam, Watergate...

Around the same time, Chinese leader Mao Zedong described the United States as a country in decline and "incapable of maintaining its hegemony over the capitalist countries."[71] In emerging countries—at that time, they were most often described as developing nations—the United States was losing influence at the expense of the Soviet Union.[72] During a 1960 flight to Tokyo, President Eisenhower's plane had to turn around midflight because the Japanese government could not guarantee the president's security due to massive student protests against American imperialism. Henry Kissinger, then a professor at Harvard University, wrote in 1961 that "only self-delusion can keep us from admitting our decline to ourselves."[73]

Next came the showdown over Russian missiles in Cuba. President John F. Kennedy faced down the Soviets and forced them to retreat—and in doing so, he brought the world to the brink of nuclear war. President Kennedy's firm stand in the Cuban Missile Crisis brought some relief to the American state of mind.

Newsweek argued that Kennedy's management of the Cuba crisis had given Americans "a deep sense of confidence in the temper of their President and the team working with him."[74] Nevertheless, the United States was unable to dislodge the Castro regime in Cuba—a fact that was impossible to hide.[75]

Around the time of the Bay of Pigs debacle, the Soviet Union dealt another major blow to American prestige and self-confidence. Early in 1961, Yuri Gagarin became the first man in space. President Kennedy sensed the importance of this event and declared that "this nation should commit itself to achieving the goal, before this decade is out, of landing a man on the moon and returning him safely to the earth."[76] In 1969, Neil Armstrong became the first man to set foot on the moon (and return safely, to boot)—a brief moment of radiance in an era of gloom.

The debacle in Vietnam, described by Harvard University professor of political science Harvey Mansfield as a "comprehensive disaster,"[77] deeply humiliated America and strengthened feelings of loss of power and decline. During the 1960s, the deep division of the nation was evident everywhere: the murders of John and Robert Kennedy and Martin Luther King, Jr., the antiwar movement, the flower-power revolt of the younger generation, and the progress of the Civil Rights Movement alongside ugly displays of racism. Rachel Carson's best seller, *Silent Spring*, documented the damage caused by pesticides, giving birth to the ecology movement.[78]

Early in the 1960s, political scientist Michael Harrington provoked intense debate by claiming that much of the United States was still an underdeveloped nation, with hidden pockets of extreme poverty.[79] Historian Allen Matusow later described the 1960s as the "Unraveling of America."[80] Soviet and Chinese leaders openly talked about American decline; even hard-liner Henry Kissinger concluded that the United States had "passed its high point like so many other civilizations," adding that he was trying "to persuade the Russians to give us the best deal we can get."[81]

During the 1970s, belief in America's decline continued to flourish. When President Nixon removed the United States from the gold standard that had formed the backbone of the post–World War II economic order, it was generally considered an unmistakable sign of sagging American economic power and resilience. Next, the Watergate scandal threatened the credibility of American institutions and values and led to Nixon's resignation in disgrace. That was followed by the 1973 oil embargo imposed by the Organization of the Petroleum Exporting Countries (OPEC) nations; the resulting oil price hikes led to recession, unemployment, inflation, and long lines at gas stations—a humiliating experience for many Americans.

Of course, the decade was also haunted by the Vietnam War. As the last American soldiers and civilians were leaving Vietnam, the leading German newspaper *Frankfurter Allgemeine Zeitung* printed a front-page editorial titled "America—A Helpless Giant."[82] In 1975, Harvard University sociologist Daniel Bell concluded,

> The American Century lasted scarcely 30 years. It foundered on the shoals of Vietnam…. There are clear signs that America is being displaced as the paramount country…. Internal tensions have multiplied and there are deep structural crises, political and cultural, that may prove more intractable to solution than the domestic economic problems.[83]

Of course, this defeat in Vietnam almost immediately triggered a complete overhaul of the American military, one that gave the US Army a new comparative advantage within a relatively short period of time.

Awareness of American vulnerability was everywhere. "For the first time since the Great Depression," British commentator

Godfrey Hodgson remarked, "many Americans began to question whether their children would live as well as they had."[84] Henry Brandon, a British journalist working in Washington, DC, described it as a sea change that Americans who had always been taught to succeed now had to learn "how to suffer failure."[85]

While the government and the people of the United States struggled, the Soviet Union seemed to be firmly in control, even extending its worldwide influence. Soviet and Cuban forces were, for example, busily installing and reinforcing puppet regimes in resource-rich Central Africa. David Reynolds argued: "America's political weakness after Watergate and Vietnam was treated by Moscow as an opportunity to expand in the third world."[86] A senior Soviet official remarked that during this period, "the world was turning in our direction."[87]

The Soviet Union was not America's only concern. After the fall of the Shah of Iran, followers of Ayatollah Khomeini seized the American embassy in Tehran and 52 Americans within it. A botched attempt to liberate the hostages made the United States look powerless and weak, as did the lack of an US response to the initial Soviet invasion of Afghanistan.

US President Jimmy Carter only further reinforced the feeling of decline by claiming at one point that "the only trend is downward."[88] Carter also delivered the famous "malaise speech" that emphasized "a crisis of confidence...that strikes at the very heart and soul and spirit of our national will."[89] Around the same time, Singapore's foreign minister R.S. Rajaratnam asked, "Who will be number one?"[90] Winston Lord, head of the Council on Foreign Relations, remarked: "Our era of predominance is over."[91] They all turned out to be wrong.

Reaganite Revival

"Feelings of decline and malaise," political scientist Samuel Huntington noted, "generated the political currents that brought Ronald Reagan to power in 1981."[92] Historian David Reynolds attributed Reagan's success to the disenchantment of Americans "with what they considered the country's moral corrosion and international decline."[93] By reaching out to right-wing groups, such as the Moral Majority, Ronald Reagan won the presidential election of 1980 with an optimistic message stressing that "government *is* not the solution to our problem; government is the problem," and "it's morning again in America" became the stickiest slogan of Reagan's 1984 reelection campaign.

Reagan succeeded in convincing Americans that the decline of the 1970s was not due to structural deficiencies in the American model but instead to a lack of true leadership and appropriate policies. He dropped containment and accommodation and faced down the Soviets with a new arms race. Historian Niall Ferguson described it as the "Reagan–[Caspar] Weinberger arms extravaganza" that not only led to the collapse of the Soviet Union but also produced a "quantum leap in military capabilities that left other powers far behind."[94] In March 1983, Ronald Reagan made very clear where he stood when describing the Soviet Union as "an evil empire...the focus of evil in the modern world...communism is another sad, bizarre chapter in human history, whose last pages even now are being written."[95]

Despite Reagan's success, declinists persisted. The United States became increasingly vulnerable to terrorist attacks; nearly 300 Americans were killed in two suicide bombings in the Lebanese capital of Beirut. But the declinists' most powerful ammunition was the meteoric rise of Japan. As early as 1979, Harvard sociologist Ezra Vogel published a book in which he argued that Japan would surpass the United States economically.[96] Michael Crichton, author of the 1992 novel *Rising Sun,* wrote that Americans had to "come to grips with the fact that Japan has become the leading industrial nation of the world."[97] It's ironic that the year

Crichton's book was published was also the first year of the longest expansion of the US economy since the mid-19th century.[98]

In 1989, the Mitsubishi group bought Rockefeller Center, a landmark in the heart of New York City. That same year, Akio Morita, chairman of the Japanese conglomerate Sony, declared that "the time will never again come when America will regain its strength in industry." Shintaro Ishihara, a former Japanese cabinet minister, added that "there is no hope for the U.S."[99] A year earlier, Clyde Prestowitz, former assistant secretary of commerce in the Reagan administration, declared that "the American Century is over"[100] and that his country was a Japanese "colony in the making."[101] Even when it was becoming obvious that Japan was facing some serious structural problems of its own—the Nikkei share index crashed, a real estate bubble exploded, and the Japanese financial system was overloaded with zombie banks—a prominent American politician declared: "The Cold War is over, and Japan won."[102] In effect, Japan had become the China of the 1970s and 1980s.

In 1987, Paul Kennedy, a British historian at Yale University, published the acclaimed *The Rise and Fall of the Great Powers*.[103] As had happened with so many great powers before them, Kennedy argued, the spiraling cost of the arms race would exhaust the economies of the Soviet Union and the United States. In his book, Kennedy meticulously investigated empire after empire, concluding that a loss of relative economic position inevitably leads to the loss of power and status. European powers of earlier centuries, for example, decayed because they consistently failed "to recognize the importance of preserving the economic underpinnings of a powerful military machine."[104]

Around the same time, a different, or at least much more nuanced, message was put forth by journalist Joel Kotkin and management consultant Yoriko Kishimoto. In their book *The Third Century*, Kotkin and Kishimoto acknowledged the rise of Japan and other strong Asian economies, such as South Korea, Taiwan, and China.[105] Yet they remained upbeat regarding the prospects of American power and dominance. Kotkin and Kishimoto referred to America's entrepreneurial culture as a unique asset, especially regarding development of products and services related to new technologies. In their view, the entrepreneurial culture was indicative of the creativity, flexibility, and daring at the essence of the American character. They also expected American entrepreneurial activity to receive a significant boost from Asian immigration into the United States. Compared to Asian and European countries, Kotkin and Kishimoto concluded, the United States still held the best cards.

Unipolar Dominance

Although major weaknesses in the Soviet system had become visible over time, only a minority believed, like German Chancellor Helmut Schmidt, that the Soviet Union was "Upper Volta with nuclear weapons."[106] In the 1960s, Nobel Prize–winning economist Paul Samuelson predicted that the Soviet economy would overtake America's by 1984. In the 1980 edition of his classic textbook *Economics,* Samuelson was still holding on to his hypothesis, but he pushed back the date to 2010.[107]

As the 1980s proceeded, however, the USSR began to crumble. The Soviets could not match Reagan's rearmament because their economic system was defunct.[108] The fall of the prices of oil and gas during the 1980s was the final nail in the Soviets' coffin; during that decade, the price of a barrel of oil plunged from $100 to $40. The Soviet state became bankrupt. Unable to reverse course, it collapsed.[109]

In 2002, Kennedy was moved to admit that never before in history had there been such an enormous disparity in power as that which existed between the United States and the rest of the world.[110] Shortly after the fall of the Soviet empire, the United

States triumphed in the first Gulf War. Democracy gained another big win in June 1989, as the world looked on in horror as the Chinese government crushed a student demonstration in Beijing's historic Tiananmen Square. Among the students' crimes: erecting a plaster Goddess of Democracy with a clear resemblance to the Statue of Liberty. Europe found itself unable to fix the nightmarish situation that developed following the breakup of Yugoslavia without help; American diplomat Richard Holbrooke finally managed to broker peace.

The declinists' opponents were giddy with pleasure. Conservative columnist Charles Krauthammer sarcastically remarked that "if the Roman Empire had declined at [our] rate, you'd be reading this column in Latin."[111]

Successes came in areas other than foreign affairs as well. During Bill Clinton's presidency, the economy boomed with close to full employment, the stock market spiraled upward, and the federal budget was balanced. French Foreign Secretary Hubert Védrine expressed what many were thinking when in 1999 he described the United States as "hyperpuissance," a kind of super superpower. This was remarkable given the long tradition of explicit anti-Americanism among the French elite;[112] a few years earlier, France's president, Jacques Chirac, told United Nations (UN) officials that "if you want to find idiotic behavior you can always count on the Americans."[113] The seeming inability of successive governments to stop Japan's slide into recession and deflation further highlighted America's relative strength.

Despite violent or diplomatic setbacks in Somalia, Bosnia, North Korea, and Haiti and the first signs of what Osama bin Laden and Al Qaeda were capable of, the 1990s made the declinists seem out of touch with reality. Before becoming president of the World Bank, Deputy Secretary of State Robert Zoellick wrote that "the vitality of America's private economy, the preeminence of its military power, and the appeal of the country's ideas are unparalleled."[114] Political scientist John Ikenberry concluded that "the preeminence of American power [is] unprecedented."[115] Amid all this triumphalism, BBC correspondent Gavin Esler shrewdly observed: "America has conquered the world and yet Americans have found little peace."[116]

However, there were dissenters in the boom years. Influential American thinkers like Samuel Huntington and Joseph Nye challenged the notion of a unipolar world dominated by America.[117] In 1992, Washington strategist Edward Luttwak described the United States as a "third-world country [going] straight downhill,"[118] and in the same year, Johns Hopkins economist David Calleo warned of America's imminent bankruptcy.[119] Massachusetts Institute of Technology (MIT) professor Lester Thurow wrote in the early 1990s of the coming economic battle among Europe, Japan, and America; according to him, the best cards were held by Europe.[120]

And Back Again, and Again…

Declinism returned with a vengeance after the bursting of the dotcom bubble in 2000. Although this did not produce the deep recession that many feared was inevitable, the terrorist attacks of 9/11, the wars in Iraq and Afghanistan, and the financial crisis and the Great Recession sank America into a morass. The British playwright Harold Pinter defined the United States in the context of 9/11 and the 2002 invasion of Iraq as "the most dangerous power the world has ever known."[121] In his Nobel Prize acceptance speech at the end of 2005, Pinter declared that "the crimes of the United States have been systematic, constant, vicious, remorseless…. [The country] has exercised…a brilliant, even witty, highly successful act of hypnosis."[122]

Several books focused on America's decline enjoyed success early in the 21st century. French social scientist Emmanuel Todd concluded in *Après l'Empire: Essai sur la Décomposition du Système*

Americain that the American system was simply falling apart.[123] Foreign affairs specialist Charles Kupchan's book *The End of the American Era* reflected an integrated Europe as the major competitor to the United States.[124] In *The United States of Europe: The New Superpower and the End of American Supremacy,* T.R. Reid described Europe as "the new superpower" bringing about "the end of American supremacy."[125] American economist Jeremy Rifkin described "how Europe's vision of the future is quietly eclipsing the American Dream" in his book *The European Dream: How Europe's Vision of the Future Is Quietly Eclipsing the American Dream.*[126] In 2008, on the eve of the financial crisis and subsequent Great Recession, political commentator and *Newsweek International* editor Fareed Zakaria saw the emergence of a post-American world. Zakaria wrote that the economic rise of "the rest" was leading to increasing political power for countries such as China, India, Brazil, Russia, and South Africa.[127] In *The Limits of Power: The End of American Exceptionalism,* retired Army colonel Andrew Bacevich blamed the country's consumer craze for its extravagant foreign policy and its structural decline.[128]

The 2008 financial crisis further intensified commentary on the decline of the United States.[129] Shortly after the fall of Lehman Brothers, Oxford University's John Gray predicted that "the era of American global leadership...is over."[130] *The New York Times* claimed, "Gone are the days, from Pax Britannica to Pax Americana, when the US and the UK made the rules that others followed."[131] Once again, a great deal of emphasis was placed on the irreversible rise of Asian nations as powerhouses.[132] Some even drew parallels between the collapse of the Soviet Union and America's prospects: "America's economy will evaporate like the morning mist."[133] Nouriel Roubini had no doubt in the summer of 2008: "It is certain that the decline of the American Empire has started."[134]

Yet in the fall of 2008, in the midst of the crisis, Scottish-born Harvard University historian Niall Ferguson warned that "commentators should always hesitate before they prophesy the decline and fall of the United States."[135] Stephen Flynn, a senior fellow at the Council on Foreign Relations, counted on "America the Resilient" in the sense that "resilience has historically been one of the United States' great strengths." Although he remained fundamentally optimistic, Flynn did caution that strong, intelligent policies were necessary in order to "allow Americans to remain true to their ideals no matter what tempest the future may bring."[136]

By early 2010, leading German weekly *Der Spiegel* published a series of articles on the United States under the general title "A Superpower in Decline." The *Spiegel* staff argued that

> the United States of 2010 is dysfunctional.... [It] is a confused and fearful country in 2010.... The Desperate States of America are loud and distressed. The country has always been a little paranoid but now it's also despondent, hopeless and pessimistic.... The country is reacting strangely irrationally to the loss of its importance—it is a reaction characterized primarily by rage. Significant portions of America simply want to... devote almost no effort to reflection, and they condemn cleverness and intellect as elitist and un-American, as if people who hunt bears could seriously be expected to lead a world power.[137]

Although an existential crisis in the Eurozone was building quickly, a sense of moral and intellectual superiority pervaded Europe by the end of the 2000s. In this respect, the *Der Spiegel* articles were representative of opinions held by many Europeans about the United States and its leadership. Kati Suominen of the German Marshall Fund of the United States remarked, the United States has become portrayed as a nation divided at home and discredited abroad, its economy sullied by deficits and stifled by disinvestment, its global primacy overtaken by a near-audible power shift from West to East. In all too common depictions, America is passing the baton of global stewardship to emerging nations. A new world order led by China is said to be waiting in the shadows.[138]

The first years of this decade were hallmarked with negativity. International investor Jim Rogers reflected: "Countries rise, and then they decline. It happened to the British and the Spanish; it happened to Egypt and Rome; it is happening to the United States."[139] *Financial Times* writer Gideon Rachman wrote an article entitled "American Decline: This Time It's Real."[140] Journalist Steven Hill concluded that for America, "the European way is the best hope in an insecure age."[141]

Yet in 2012, the tide of declinist feelings and writings began to reverse, at least to some degree. Europe was paralyzed by a seemingly insolvable crisis in the Eurozone, and the European Union was faced off against Vladimir Putin's Russia. Japan found itself unable to combat stagnation and deflation despite a huge increase in its government debt. The Chinese economic system was starting to show signs of severe strain. But the United States was climbing out of the Great Recession better and faster than most analysts had predicted.

Daniel Gross published a book on America's economy with the title *Better, Stronger, Faster.*[142] *The Economist* ran a story called "The Comeback Kid" that, not surprisingly, commented positively on the prospects of the American economy: "Old weaknesses are being remedied and new strengths discovered, with an agility that has much to teach stagnant Europe and dirigiste Asia."[143] Bill Emmott, former editor of *The Economist,*[144] concluded in an article titled "The

American Century Is Not Over" that the time had come to "rethink all the fashionable assumptions about America's decline."[145]

In 2013, Ely Ratner of the Center for a New American Society and Thomas Wright of the Brookings Institution wrote a remarkable op-ed piece in the *Washington Post* titled, "America's Not in Decline—It's on the Rise." Ratner and Wright argued,

> The United States is experiencing a turnaround of fortunes…. In terms of hard power, the US military is at the forefront of next-generation technologies, including unmanned systems, robotics and lasers. Even more superior than its hardware is its software: the command and control systems to conduct highly advanced joint operations and major wars…. The United States also remains the linchpin of the international community. Through hard-nosed diplomacy, economic pressure and the specter of military action, Washington has retained its ability to marshal effective multinational coalitions…. More broadly, and most importantly, the United States is blessed with a superior combination of sound fundamentals in demography, geography, higher education and innovation.[146]

The Necessary Condition

America's decline has been predicted almost continuously since the country was created; this is a remarkable thing to note, of course, but it doesn't say anything about the present or a future situation. Just because it was proven wrong again and again doesn't mean that next time, it will be proven false again.

But the basic point of *A Giant Reborn* is that it will indeed be proven wrong again. Despite what may be seen as appearances to the contrary, the evidence convincingly points toward continued American dominance; this evidence can be divided into internal and external elements.

In order to become and remain a dominant player on the world stage, a country or a region must have considerable economic power. I agree with *The Economist*'s conclusion that "in the end it is the health of a country's economy that determines its faith."[147] This is, of course, not a novel insight. Paul Kennedy was one of the first to put forth this argument, and many others followed in his footsteps.[148] You can't build military strength or far-reaching diplomatic influence with limited or declining economic power. After all, what brought the Soviet Union down? A complete economic collapse, hastened by an accelerated arms race under Reagan.[149]

I'm not arguing that economic strength is a *sufficient* condition to achieve world dominance. My point is that it is a *necessary* condition. If an economic metric—say gross domestic product—were relevant regarding power, the EU would have surpassed the United States years ago. In world affairs, power is often divided in two groups: hard and soft. Both kinds matter, and for both, enduring economic power is a necessary condition. I concur with Kennedy's stress on a strong economy and extend his idea in two directions. First, I consider what lies beneath that economic resilience, and second, I determine what else is necessary—beyond economic performance—to stay at the top.[150]

Any real competition for the top power spot would have to come up with a truly attractive alternative to the capitalist world order, which, in the words of political scientist Michael Mandelbaum, is built on the principles of peace, democracy, and free markets.[151]

Internally, the United States still possesses impressive strengths. It is still by far the largest economy in the world. Josef Joffe noted that in 2012, the United States' economy led those of contenders like China and the EU by a wider margin than is generally accepted.[152] In addition, the United States is best poised for economic growth in the coming decades simply because it is best equipped to deal with change in the broadest sense of the word. The technological, economic, social, and political developments expected to occur during the coming decades will cause change to happen faster and more intensely than ever before. I describe this as *turbochange*. The next few decades, I predict, will be an extreme illustration of the Greek proverb "nothing endures but change."

The growing knowledge base possessed by human capital, the worldwide entrepreneurial drive typical of the 21st century so far, and globalization are among the dynamic forces behind turbochange. Along with turbochange's strong economic performance will come drawbacks, including tensions and major upheaval in society. Change means progress, but also disruption of existing equilibria, as it inevitably produces winners and losers. If anything, the divide between the winners and losers will become larger as time progresses. The fight to hang on to privilege will become increasingly intense and may lead to societal disruption. Thus, my belief that the United States is best equipped to deal with turbochange is an analytical conclusion, not an ethical evaluation of the American model. Other societies might deal with turbochange in another way than America and, as a whole, feel better about it. But in the long run, the American system performs best in terms of economic strength and the creation of geopolitical power.

It's no coincidence that the United States is so well suited for turbochange, as innovation—the basis of most change—is aggressively sought after on its shores. Joseph Schumpeter's notion of creative destruction—a key component of successful capitalism—is a necessary condition for a thriving economy like that of the United States. Capitalist economies derail from time to time and produce excesses, like financial bubbles, on a regular basis. Because the institutional and societal setup of the United States is so strong, the economy bounces back and regains strength each time. A perfect example is taking place now in the field of energy production—shale oil and gas.

Continuously strong economic performance creates the opportunity for great powers to make bad decisions (e.g., in terms of military issues) and get away with it. Their economic resilience gives them ample room to correct the consequences of mistakes and bad judgment, but only so far. A continuous string of lousy decisions will start to weigh on any economy. Strong economic powers can behave stupidly, but only for a limited amount of time, and to a manageable degree. Consider the example of the Soviet Union.

The external component? That would be an analysis of the economic and political futures of America's primary competitors. China, the EU and other economies may be well poised, but at the same time, they face problems of their own. In Chapter 4, I further develop this argument for China and Europe. More often than not, these problems undermine a country or region's capacity to deal with change. Specifically, interest groups have a greater impact on policy directions than in the United States. Strong pressure to maintain the status quo in China and the EU leads to systematic blocking of creative destruction, thus undermining economic growth. This clear disadvantage is caused by historic, social, political, and economic factors.

Chapter 2

The Dynamics of Turbochange

"There are *known knowns:* there are things we know
that we know. There are *known unknowns:* that is to say,
there are things that we now know we don't know. But
there are also *unknown unknowns:* there are things we
do not know we don't know."

—Donald Rumsfeld, US Secretary of Defense,
February 12, 2002

RUMSFELD MADE THESE REMARKS WHILE BEING QUES-
tioned about the possible role of the Iraqi government
in supplying weapons of mass destruction to terrorist
groups. His now-legendary words have applications to the topic
of American decline (or, more appropriately, American rebirth).
Rumsfeld's quote is key to understanding the argument in favor of
continued American resilience and dominance.

The known knowns Rumsfeld referred to are, of course, basic
truths and regularities, like the law of gravity, the boiling point
of water, or election results in North Korea. One of these eternal
truths—a known known—is that tomorrow will be different from
today. "If history teaches us nothing else," investor Jim Rogers

wrote, "it teaches us this: what appears undisputed today will look very different tomorrow."[153]

As far as political, military, economic, social, cultural, and/or technological evolutions are concerned, we can take for granted that important shifts will occur. Historical regularities and human nature guarantee this outcome. Change is the known known *par excéllence*. But, unfortunately, we can't predict what that change will look like.

When it comes to certain change, the known unknowns are those things we know for sure will change, but for which multiple outcomes are possible—perhaps even outcomes that we cannot possibly predict. We won't know how quickly or slowly change will come, how it will work out in different countries or regions, and what its consequences to society will be. We can make educated guesses about the next steps forward (or backward) that can be expected in, say, medical technology, the democratization process in Russia or China, the development of new energy sources, the quest for worldwide recognition of basic human rights, the evolution of the EU, the ways to deal with climate change, the fight against murderous extremism, and so on. These and so many other important issues will evolve and will beyond any doubt look very different in the future. We do, however, not know *how* different—hence, known unknowns.

The Reality of Unknowns

There exists a gray field between Rumsfeld's known unknowns and his unknown unknowns. Where is the line between something you know is going to change but don't know how or how much and something you really can't imagine at all? The interaction between humans and machines is a good example. Google's director of engineering, inventor and futurist Ray Kurzweil, has delivered spectacular forecasting of the way in which humans and machines will interact and coexist in the future. This interaction, he claims, will merge biology and technology to, among other things, overcome age-old human problems and enormously increase human creativity.[154] Within the same context, science writer Michael Chorost wrote *World Wide Mind*, a fascinating book on the progress made in direct mind-to-mind communication, a subject that was previously nothing more than science fiction.[155]

There are known unknowns in these fields, but also unknown unknowns. We can be absolutely sure that research in the fields of human and technological interaction will lead to things, material or otherwise, that we cannot foresee (unknown unknowns). Other things will be developed that are similar to things currently in existence, yet very different than those we currently have (known unknowns). This is true for other fields as well. For example, it is virtually certain that in the fields of food production, energy, and communication technology, there will be developments that most of us, if not all of us, cannot remotely imagine today.

The World Economic Forum (WEF), the organization behind the yearly high-level meetings in the Swiss resort city of Davos, publishes a yearly list of the top ten emerging technologies. Its Top 10 for 2014, which makes for fascinating reading, is led by "body-adapted wearable electronics."[156] According to the WEF's technology panel, "body-adapted electronics…will further push the ever-shifting boundary between humans and technology," with "hundreds of millions of devices [to be] in use by 2016."[157] Next on the WEF's list are "nanostructured carbon composites" that can address several problems that have hampered the use of carbon fiber in cars and other vehicles. These carbon composites could have a major impact, the WEF's panel concludes, "by bringing forward the potential for manufacturing lightweight, super-safe and recyclable composite vehicles to a mass scale."[158]

Number three is "mining metals from desalination brine." The worldwide shortage of fresh water can potentially be solved by desalination of sea water. A major problem with desalination is that it leaves a "reject-concentrated brine which can have a serious impact on marine life when returned to the sea."[159] New technologies based on catalyst-assisted chemistry suggest that the waste brine can yield valuable elements, such as lithium, magnesium, uranium, sodium, potassium, and calcium, thereby reducing desalination's negative environmental impact.

In a similar vein, the McKinsey Global Institute examined "disruptive technologies, advances that will transform life, business and the global economy."[160] Its list includes new Internet developments, the internet of things, cloud technology, advanced robotics, energy storage, 3D printing, and next-generation genomics. McKinsey strongly emphasizes the fact that the speed of change in these fields is becoming faster and faster, and that combinations of new technologies with other new technologies will likely lead to more unknown unknowns, innovations we cannot presently comprehend.[161] For example, some analysts predict a "resource revolution," or greatly increased productivity in the use of natural resources, that will arise through a combination of tools and methods provided by information technology, biology, and nanotechnology.[162]

As fascinating as the WEF's top 10 and McKinsey's analysis of disruptive technologies are, it's worth considering that at this very moment, emerging technologies exist that aren't on either list. The fact that several items on the WEF's list do not appear in the McKinsey list, and vice versa, is a perfect illustration of this. The history of technological progress is littered with the element of surprise—once more: unknown unknowns.

Also, some of these technologies will prove to be wildly overrated, and others wildly underrated. Consider laser technology.[163] One of the technology's innovators described the initial reaction to its discovery in the late 1950s and early 1960s as "a solution looking for a problem."[164] Of course, the laser has become a broadly used technology that is clearly beneficial to human progress.

A more recent example is the history of the personal computer. When it was first developed, IBM's leadership saw only a very limited market for the PC. As one IBM insider argued: "Why on earth would you care about a personal computer? It has nothing to do with automation. It isn't a product for big companies that use 'real' computers."[165]

In other cases, time has proven to be the deciding factor. Ever since the concept of robotics was introduced in 1941, expectations were high. Yet *The Economist* concluded early in 2014 that so far,

> they have not yet made much of a mark on the world.... That seems to be about to change. Exponential growth in the power of silicon chips, digital sensors, and high-bandwidth communications has improved the prospects for robotics just as it has improved those for all sorts of other products.[166]

Likewise, the autonomous vehicle took time. A DARPA project to develop one began in 2002 and seemed to go nowhere for years. *Popular Science* published an article in 2004 entitled "DARPA's Debacle in the Desert."[167] In 2005, economists Frank Levy and Richard Murnane argued in their book *The New Division of Labor: How Computers Are Creating the Next Job Market* that driving a car was too complex a task for a computer to ever be capable of handling.[168] Google's Chauffeur software had become so sophisticated by 2010 that its autonomous cars could function in real-life traffic situations.

So, technology follows an unpredictable path of progress and advancement. Despite endless evidence of this, some still refuse to believe that technological progress will always continue. And whether or not you believe in progress has a tremendous impact on your perspective on the future of humanity. Former *Business Week* chief economist Michael Mandel once argued that "...technology-driven growth is essential...if we are not to drown in our own problems…. Without rapid economic growth powered by new technologies, it won't be possible to reduce poverty or ensure the next generation a better life than we have."[169]

This book is firmly rooted in an optimistic future filled with technological advancement and continuous economic growth. Technological progress produces productivity gains, which drive economic growth. Nobel Prize–winning economist Paul Krugman remarked, "productivity isn't everything, but in the long run it is almost everything."[170] My belief in further technological advancement is anchored in a dispassionate analysis of the determinants of human progress.

The End of the Line?

So I am an optimist. Pessimists who have written contrary opinions about just how much impact, in terms of real human progress, future technological and scientific advancements will hold, include economists Tyler Cowen and Robert Gordon; medical scientist Jan Vijg; biotech environmentalist Michael Huesemann; chess master and Russian political activist Garry Kasparov and high-tech entrepreneurs Max Levchin and Peter Thiel; and philosophers Martin Heidegger and Jacques Ellul.[171] In 2014, Nobel Prize–winning economist Joseph Stiglitz joined these contrarians in an opinion piece entitled "The Innovation Enigma." Stiglitz wrote, "one cannot avoid the uneasy feeling that, when all is said and done, the contribution of recent technological innovations to long-term growth in living standards may be substantially less than the enthusiasts claim."[172]

Pessimism about the potential of future technological progress is deeply embedded in the ecological movement. This explains to a large extent why, for example, the global think tank Club of Rome regularly predicts the coming exhaustion of natural resources. Yet constant development of new technology and the tendency of human behavior to adapt as environment and incentives change have proven their projections wrong time and again. Each time the Club launches a new prediction, it argues that this time around, it will come true because "based on what we know today," technological progress and changed incentives will not and cannot come to the rescue.[173] Well.

The following quote from Robert Gordon, a professor of economics at Northwestern University, summarizes technology pessimism and a belief in vanishing economic growth:

> Since Solow's seminal work in the 1950s, economic growth has been regarded as a continuous process that will persist forever. But there was virtually no economic growth before 1750, suggesting that the rapid progress made over the past 250 years could well be a unique episode in human history rather than a guarantee of endless future advance at the same rate.... The frontier established by the US for output per capita, and the U.K. before it, gradually began to grow more rapidly after 1750, reached its fastest growth rate in the middle of the 20th century, and has slowed since. It is in the process of slowing down further.[174]

Tyler Cowen, an economist at George Mason University, echoes this analysis. He does not see how information and communication technology, the Internet, and other related technologies will be able to create productivity increases like those experienced in the past with, for example, the advents of the steam engine, electricity, and mass transport. The availability of open land in the United States and impressive advances in education have created lots of "low-hanging fruit," according to Cowen. Thus, Cowen's argument leads to rather pessimistic conclusions:

> We are failing to understand why we are failing. All of [our] problems have a single, little-noticed root cause: We have been living off low-hanging fruit for at least

two hundred years.... Yet during the last forty years, that low-hanging fruit started disappearing, and we started pretending it was still there. We have failed to recognize that we are at a technological plateau and the trees are more bare than we would like to think.... We have built social and economic institutions on the expectation of a lot of low-hanging fruit, but that fruit is mostly gone.[175]

Even an optimist like Angus Deaton, Princeton's *éminence grise* health economist, has doubts: "Perhaps the gods of technical change have abandoned us."[176]

...No Way

But there are plenty of optimists who think like me, including journalist Matt Ridley, historian Joel Mokyr, economists Martin Baily of the Brookings Institution and James Manyika and Shalab Gupta of consulting giant McKinsey; MIT's Center for Digital Business scholars Erik Brynjolfsson and Andrew McAfee; economists Martin Weitzman and Paul Romer; and the late economist Julian Simon.[177] Harvard's Edward Glaeser and MIT's Daron Acemoglu, two of the most outstanding economists of the moment, are also in this camp. Even the great John Maynard Keynes was optimistic when contemplating the economic future of his grandchildren at the start of the Great Depression.[178]

Yet this optimism is not blind, unconditional adulation. New technologies will probably create important and difficult-to-resolve issues for society at large.[179] For example, technological advancement has been an important driving force behind the growth of income inequality in the industrialized world—an issue that is creeping toward the top of policy agendas in more and more countries.[180] There's also the effect of technological evolution on the democratic process. Technology can become an instrument of repression: for example, "the dark side of Internet freedom."[181]

The argument for optimism regarding future technological advancement has origins in basic human nature and characteristics, and the way humans interact with each other and their environment. Science writer Michael Chorost writes of a push–pull dynamic that

> has rammed innovation into overdrive.... Plows led to better harvests, which gave people leisure time to invent better plows. Telegraphs let newspapers go national, which created a demand for better journalistic tools such as teletypewriters. New computer chips let electrical engineers create even faster chips. Each push triggers a pull, which sets the stage for another push.[182]

Paul Romer, a leading researcher on economic growth, also argues against the Club of Rome's fatalism, stating that

> every generation has perceived limits to growth that finite resources and undesirable side effects would pose if no new recipes and ideas were discovered. And every generation has underestimated the potential for finding new recipes and ideas. We consistently fail to grasp how many new ideas remain to be discovered.[183]

In his superb book *The Rational Optimist,* Matt Ridley writes,

> So long as human exchange and specialization are allowed to thrive somewhere, then culture evolves whether leaders help it or hinder it, and the result is that prosperity spreads, technology progresses, poverty declines, disease retreats, fecundity falls, happiness increases, violence atrophies, freedom grows, knowledge flourishes, the environment improves and wilderness expands.[184]

Brynjolfsson and McAfee agree: "We're living in a time of astonishing progress with digital technologies [and] the transformations brought about by digital technologies will be profoundly beneficial ones."[185] Daron Acemoglu, another highly regarded scholar from MIT, sees

> little evidence that we are running out of innovations. This is not only so because there are literally millions of ideas that can be recombined into new ones to generate new processes and products, but also because every innovation poses new problems and opens the way for yet more innovations, as illustrated most recently by smart phones, tablets and social media, which have created new industries centered on developing applications for these platforms.[186]

Northwestern University economic historian Joel Mokyr and Harvard's Edward Glaeser point to information technology as a very important ingredient of the optimist view on the world of innovation and progress. Glaeser argues,

> In many ways, information technology makes innovation itself easier by easing the flow of ideas. Much research today uses tools like Google, JSTOR, Wikipedia, and STATA. Information technology enables experimentation and evaluation, which speed the creation of knowledge itself. It stores information to ensure that our stock of knowledge continues to grow, contributing to an ongoing increase in worldwide wealth.[187]

Mokyr adds an important historical aspect to Glaeser's argument:

> There is no automatic mechanism that turns better science into improved technology. But there is one reason to believe that in the near future it will do so better and more efficiently than ever before. The reason is access. Inventors, engineers, applied chemists, and physi-

cians all need access to best-practice science to answer an infinite list of questions about what can and cannot be done. Search engines were invented in the 18th century through encyclopaedias and compendia that arranged all available knowledge in alphabetical order, making it easy to find. Textbooks had indices that did the same. Libraries developed cataloguing systems and other techniques that made scientific information findable. But these search systems have their limitations. One might have feared that the explosion of scientific knowledge in the 20th century could outrun our ability to find what we are looking for. Yet the reverse has happened. The development of searchable databanks of massive sizes has even outrun our ability to generate scientific knowledge.[188]

Big Data—the idea that more and more data can be analyzed with increasingly powerful tools and methods—offers enormous potential for improvement and discovery.[189]

On to Turbochange

I'd add to Chorost's push–pull dynamic, Ridley's optimism, and Mokyr's and Glaeser's access arguments that both the known unknowns and unknown unknowns surrounding mankind will continue to evolve even faster than before and in more unexpected ways than before. German executive Reinhard Mohn, the founder of the Bertelsmann Foundation, wrote, "Already in the twentieth century change has taken place with unprecedented speed. But it will become even faster due to increase in knowledge and its ready availability."[190]

Humanity is shifting from an environment in continuous change to one in turbochange. Ian Morris, a history professor at Stanford University, wrote a brilliant grand theory of human history in *Why the West Rules—For Now*. "For millennia," Morris argued, "social development has generally been increasing, thanks to our tinkering, *and has generally done so at an accelerating rate* [italics mine]. Good ideas beget more good ideas, and having once had good ideas we tend not to forget them."[191]

In his book *The Nature of Technology,* Santa Fe Institute economist, engineer, and mathematician W. Brian Arthur described a process of cumulative knowledge resulting in an increasing degree of technological advancement.[192] When arguing that we constantly failed to see that new ideas would keep on coming, Paul Romer adds that "possibilities do not merely add up, *they multiply* [italics mine]."[193]

Of course, there's nothing new about these ideas. For example, in the early 1920s, the American sociologist William Fielding Ogburn (1886–1959) saw technological advances as the primary engine of human progress.[194] In his book *Social Change with Respect to Culture and Original Nature,* Ogburn predicted that an increase in technological knowledge would inevitably lead to a boom in inventions and innovations. Ogburn also foresaw that societal responses to these innovations could become obstacles to them, coining the term "cultural lag" for the time it takes for society to catch up with and adjust to technology. One of my main arguments in Chapter 3 is that cultural lag in the United States is relatively shorter than those in Europe and Asia due to a combination of historical, political, social, and economic factors.

For a great illustration of turbochange, look to Moore's law. In 1965, Gordon Moore, the cofounder of Intel, predicted that, based on previous advancements in integrated circuit technology, one would be able to buy double the amount of computing power for the same money from one year to the next.[195] This meant that by 1975, the amount of computing power available for $1 would be 500 times greater than the amount available in 1965. And that is exactly what has happened, despite continuous predictions about the demise of Moore's law.[196]

An example like Moore's law doesn't necessarily prove that turbochange will occur with rigorous regularity. In their book *Good Capitalism, Bad Capitalism and the Economics of Growth and Prosperity*, Baumol, Litan, and Schramm wrote, "Radical innovations and the changes they spawn have a tendency to come in waves."[197] Periods of extremely rapid change will alternate with periods of much slower change. There will be many mistakes and false starts as scientific and technological progress do not always take place along an upward-sloping curve. Perhaps Mario Livio, an astrophysicist at the Space Telescope Science Institute in Baltimore, put it best, saying that blunders are not only unavoidable, they form an intrinsic part of the path toward further progress.[198]

Over longer periods—say, at least a decade—I believe that change will tend to be more intense than in the preceding period. Increased uncertainty and unpredictability will surely come with this flow of not only more but also more acute change. When Jeffrey Immelt, the chairman of General Electric, calls on his managers to "become system thinkers who are comfortable with ambiguity," it's clear that turbochange is at the core of his request.[199]

Three phenomena—increasing levels of knowledge (via human capital), a worldwide drive for and by entrepreneurship, and globalization—are key to turbochange becoming an ongoing reality. I like to refer to them as the "earthly trinity." The remainder of this chapter covers each of these phenomena in more depth.

The turbochange brought about by the forces of the earthly trinity will lead to broad changes in society. There can be no doubt that they will create major opportunities in terms of human welfare and well-being. At the same time, they will also present major threats and inconveniences.

Of course, many will oppose turbochange's outcomes, and some of this opposition will be very intense and radical. Many are familiar with the term "Luddite" only as it is applied to a person who avoids technology, but are unfamiliar with its origin. The term refers to a movement in Britain that took place from 1811 to 1817. During this time, a group of traditional textile artisans—Luddites—tried to destroy machinery that they feared would destroy their trade and jobs.[200] So it is that Luddites of the future will fear and will try to block progress.

The "Residual"

The first element of the earthly trinity is knowledge as embodied in human capital. The concept of human capital has been around since the beginning of economic theory. The work of economists like William Petty (1623–1687), Adam Smith (1723–1790), Leon Walras (1834–1910), and Irving Fisher (1867–1947) contains traces of what we consider today to be the theory of human capital.[201] During the 1960s, Kenneth Arrow[202] and Donald Keesing introduced the concept of human capital in the theory of international trade.[203]

The theory of human capital became a core part of standard economic theory primarily due to the work of three economists: Jacob Mincer (1922–2006), Theodore W. Schultz (1902–1998), and Gary Becker (1930–2014). Schultz and Becker's contribution to the theory of human capital was the deciding factor in their win of the Nobel Prize in economics. For a time, all three were colleagues at the University of Chicago, and Mincer and Becker were also together at Columbia University during the 1960s.[204]

Human capital has been defined in different ways. Some have referred to it as "knowledge, competency, attitude and behavior embedded in an individual"; others see it as "an investment that people make in themselves to increase their productivity."[205] Former Federal Reserve chairman Ben Bernanke and his coauthor Robert Frank defined human capital as "an amalgam of factors such as education, experience, training, intelligence, energy, work habits, trustworthiness, and initiative that affect the value of the worker's marginal product."[206] For this analysis, I define human capital as the stock of knowledge embodied in people that is available for humanity to use in productive and entrepreneurial activities.[207] Between 1948 and 1984 in the United States, the value of the stock of human capital was estimated as five to ten times higher than the value of the stock of physical capital.[208] In *A Giant Reborn,* I use the terms "knowledge" and "human capital" interchangeably. Here, my emphasis is on the importance of human capital in the process of economic growth.

The theory of economic growth had come a long way before human capital entered its lexicon. Although efforts to come to grips with the phenomena of growth and advancement were evident as far back as Adam Smith, MIT economist and Nobel Prize winner Robert Solow developed what came to be known as the neoclassical growth model, the first workhorse of modern growth theory.[209] One of Solow's major findings was that empirically, only a small part of experienced economic growth can be attributed to the accumulation of physical capital and labor. The most influential growth model at the time of Solow's research, the so-called Harrod–Domar model,[210] held that capital accumulation and the savings that made these capital investments possible were the crucial driver of economic growth.

Human capital did not figure in Solow's neoclassical model. He concluded that the part of economic growth not explained by the accumulation of physical capital and labor (the largest part of growth experienced to that point) was due to "the residual," or factor productivity—basically, the efficiency with which capital and labor were used. Solow further suggested that the residual was mainly driven by technological advancement.

Emphasis on technological advancement as a major driver of economic growth was not a new idea. At the end of the 1930s, the great Joseph Schumpeter claimed, "innovation...is largely responsible for most of what we would at first sight attribute to other factors"; it was obvious from the context that technological advancement was the heart of that innovative process.[211] In a 1952 article intended as an overview of current thinking on economic growth, Moses Abramovitz wrote that "technical improvement" is responsible for "a very large share, if not the bulk, of the increase in output."[212] Abramovitz emphasized the importance of both "knowledge capital" and positive externalities (to which I'll return soon).

On the heels of the development of the theory and empirics of the neoclassical growth model, some very interesting historical research on the path of technological advancement took place.[213] This research further emphasized the role of technological progress—Solow's residual—in the process of economic growth and added two key points to the neoclassical growth model: first, the technological advancement that seemed so important for the growth process took shape outside of the economic system, and second, most of the technological advancement was embodied in new capital. This research was performed in labs, universities, and other institutions outside the economic realm, leading the neoclassical growth model to be characterized as the exogenous growth theory.

As to the idea that most of the technological advancement was embodied in new capital—the ability to invest, and to invest massively, became the major objective of growth-promoting policies. This argument also implied that big institutions capable of mass production and mass investment were needed to sustain high growth levels. Early on in the 1940s, Schumpeter recognized that "what we have to accept is that the large-scale establishment or unit of control has come to be the most powerful engine of progress and in particular of the long-run expansion of output."[214] Logically, then, large entities run by highly skilled organizational and managerial experts were the surest way to reach sustained economic growth.[215] Adam Smith's "invisible hand" regulating the free market came to be replaced by what business historian Alfred Chandler called the "visible hand of the managerial revolution."[216]

Just as with human capital, entrepreneurship was not really on the radar of the neoclassical growth model. That said, several researchers did recognize its importance: Abramovitz argued in 1952 that "the role of enterprise has been slighted by traditional theory because of the theory's generally static character which easily leads to assumptions about perfect knowledge, and rational calculation of profit."[217]

For most, however, the conclusions offered by the neoclassical growth model were just a few steps away from the idea that the Soviet central-planning type economies would prove more efficient than Western decentralized market economies, because state planning allowed concentration of economic assets on a scale unthinkable in the democratic West.

An Inside Job

The idea that the neoclassical economic growth model assumed technological advancement to be exogenous (i.e., taking shape outside the economic system) soon came to be criticized. If, as Solow and others devoted to the neoclassical growth model concluded, economic growth was mainly caused by improvement in factor productivity, or overall productivity in the economy, and these productivity increases were in their turn due to technological progress, then where did these advances in technology come from? Did they fall out of the sky into a more or less receptive economic system, or was that economic environment more important than the model assumed? Was economic growth really more endogenous and less exogenous to the economic system?

The University of Chicago's Theodore W. Schultz noted in 1961 that arguing that economic growth is driven by "something," a "residual," and then describing this as "resource productivity" "gives a name to our ignorance but does not dispel it."[218] In his work as an agricultural economist, Schultz had come to important conclusions about Solow's residual:

> We were discovering that most of the increases in agricultural production during the 1940s and 1950s were occurring with no corresponding increases in land and physical inputs, and with literally fewer people…30–40 percent of the total increase in production was unexplained. It turned out that the quality of people was increasing; so, too, for physical inputs. If you stepped back, you saw it: skills were increasing and health was improving, although we weren't able to measure it in the beginning.[219]

The human capital revolution was real. The "ignorance" Schultz had lamented was about to be dispelled.

Human capital, the knowledge embodied by people as individuals or in groups, thus became the cornerstone of efforts to explain economic growth as endogenous, rather than exogenous. Technological advancement and resource productivity are not "things" that just happen to the economic system. Instead, they are driven by the system and its institutional characteristics.

Core to the turnaround in point of view was the insight that human capital is different from physical capital and unskilled labor, the traditional factors of production. As Kenneth Arrow emphasized in a groundbreaking 1962 article, knowledge is non-excludable and nonexhaustible.[220] Capital invested in one machine can't be used for other purposes, and a laborer working on a farm cannot simultaneously drive a truck from Buffalo to New York City. These restrictions simply don't hold for knowledge or human capital. Once knowledge exists and circulates, no one can be excluded from using it and no one can use it in a way that renders it unusable by others.

These characteristics of human capital lead to what economists define as externalities. The concept of externalities was introduced by Alfred Marshall (1842–1924), the doyen of neoclassical economics, but Marshall's successor at the University of Cambridge,

Arthur Pigou (1877–1959), gave the subject its first thorough treatment.[221] Externalities occur when the production or the welfare of individuals or groups increases as a consequence of actions that were not performed by those same individuals or groups, and when these effects are not priced through the market. Externalities can be positive or negative. A good example of a negative externality is pollution, as polluters are often not directly held responsible for the damage and inconveniences caused by their actions.[222]

Knowledge and human capital produce important positive externalities; some call them significant *knowledge spillovers.* During the 1980s, researchers began to analyze the contributions of these knowledge spillovers to the process of economic growth. The University of Chicago in particular yielded many seminal contributions that followed Schultz and Becker's work. Human capital theory led to the development of the endogenous growth theory, and Nobel Prize winner Robert Lucas focused on the externalities produced by human capital itself.[223] Paul Romer, who was a doctoral candidate at the University of Chicago during the 1980s, identified important externalities evident in the accumulation of knowledge yielded by companies' research and development (R&D) processes.[224] Romer's pioneering research showed that economic growth is largely driven by development of new ideas.[225] Harvard economist Martin Weitzman developed his theory of "recombinant growth" based on these insights: "In the early stages of development, growth is constrained by the number of potential new ideas, later on it is constrained by the ability to process them."[226]

More Leads to Even More

The endogenous growth models pioneered by Lucas and Romer fundamentally changed the thinking on policies with respect to economic growth. During the decades before the neoclassical growth model, and even during its heyday—say, the 1960s and

1970s—capital investment was considered the main driver of the growth process. Some recognized the importance of technology, but it was presumed to be only in the "hardware" investments. Endogenous growth models shifted the attention to the "software": investments in knowledge and human capital. This insight had huge implications, including in economic policymaking. It would, however, take another decade or two before most understood that even massive investments in knowledge and human capital needed a little something extra to become drivers of economic growth. That "something extra" was—and is—entrepreneurship, the second driver of turbochange.

Scholarship on the role of human capital externalities and knowledge spillovers has revealed that they have a huge influence in society. For example, in 1969, social scientist Jane Jacobs concluded that cities play a decisive role in the overall economic development of a country.[227] The reason? Cities facilitate much of the knowledge spillover or human capital externalities that are so critical to economic growth. Jacobs' analysis was expanded by Edward Glaeser, who stressed the

> urban ability to create collaborative brilliance.... Cities...have been engines of innovation since Plato and Socrates bickered in an Athenian marketplace. The streets of Florence gave us the Renaissance, and the streets of Birmingham gave us the Industrial Revolution.... In America and Europe, cities speed innovation by connecting their smart inhabitants to each other, but cities play an even more critical role in the developing world: They are the gateways between markets and cultures.[228]

Likewise, Michael Porter of Harvard Business School created an analysis of the competitive advantage of nations that focused on the formation of geographical clusters of activities that facilitate the spontaneous flow of positive externalities.[229]

History has proven that accumulation of human capital and knowledge is extremely important to the advancement of society in general and the process of economic growth in particular.[230] In most analyses of economic growth, it is assumed that using productive resources usually leads to decreasing returns to scale. This hypothesis implies, for example, that adding workers to a specific field in an agricultural area or to a specific industrial machine increases agricultural or industrial production, *but that it does so at a decreasing rate.* The more workers are added, the lower the increase in production will be, because the most productive units tend to be employed first. Constant returns to scale occur if each person added to the production process leads to an increase in production equal to the increase caused by adding others before or after her.

In a society dominated first by agricultural production and then by industrial production, the hypothesis of decreasing returns makes sense. Given a certain technology, adding labor and/or capital to the ongoing production process increases production, but at a decreasing rate. If human capital becomes an increasingly important factor of production, this regularity breaks down.[231] Because of substantial positive externalities, increasing amounts of human capital tend to produce increasing returns to scale.[232] I gauge these increasing returns from the societal point of view much more than from the individual point of view, as people with higher levels of knowledge are able to achieve higher levels of income.[233]

As more and more people become involved in the production and transmission of human capital, the rate of development of additional human capital tends to increase as well. Daniel Cohen, professor of economics at Paris University, wrote, "The production of new ideas or works of the mind flourishes all the more thanks to the number of researchers and artists who participate.... China has 60 million pianists; its chances of producing a new Mozart are commensurate with that figure."[234]

The development of positive externalities from knowledge and human capital are of course crucial to this process. And as more people become involved in the creation of human capital, the more specialization will occur. As more specialization occurs, more potentially innovative discoveries will be made. This human capital–driven dynamic led Brink Lindsey, a senior fellow at the Cato Institute, to suggest that it would be advisable to replace the concept of capitalism with "human capitalism."[235]

Paul Romer stressed the importance of "increasing returns that arise from the accumulation of knowledge" and "externalities [arising] because of spillovers of knowledge."[236] The exponential possibilities that modern communication technologies offer for instantaneous interaction on a worldwide scale—e-mail, video-conferencing, cloud-based file-sharing platforms, and so on—play a key role in the development of human capital. Researchers at General Electric discern the existence of "the Global Brain…essentially the collective intelligence of human beings across the globe, integrated by digital computer networks."[237]

Likewise, the level of usable products and services that can be developed from the existing and expanding stocks of human capital also tends to rise at an increasing rate. More human capital leads to still more human capital, and also to more applications that can be derived from the available stock of human capital. Here, the speed with which innovation and new technology can translate into bringing new products and services to market and increasing productivity becomes critical. That's where entrepreneurship and globalization, the other two parts of the earthly trinity, come in.

"The Single Most Important Player"

Entrepreneurship is necessary in order to reap the benefits of increasing returns on knowledge and human capital for society as a whole. The failure of the European communist bloc highlighted just how important entrepreneurship is to maximizing human capital. As eminent scholars Baumol, Litan, and Schramm noted:

> Before the Berlin Wall fell (and even since), the countries belonging to the former Soviet Union and many of the Eastern European countries boasted some of the most successful primary, secondary, and even higher-level educational systems in the world. But these systems were embedded in a political and economic atmosphere—socialism or communism—that was the very antithesis of entrepreneurship.[238]

Joel Mokyr and Aldo Schiavone, and many other historians, have long documented the ingenuity of the great civilizations of history—the Greeks, the Romans, the Chinese, to name a few. These societies innovated new techniques and tools critical to the rise of mankind, such as road building, sewers, gears, pulleys, and many more. Most of these civilizations (particularly the Romans) focused the use of these inventions on military applications; broad civilian use was less important. As Aldo Schiavone concluded,

> the famed Roman "pragmatism" was social, not technological. It affected matters of government, politics, law, and military organization.... None of the great engineers and architects, none of the incomparable builders of bridges, roads, and aqueducts, none of the experts in the employment of the apparatus of war, and none of their customers, either in the public administration or in the large landowning families, understood that the most advantageous arena for the use and improvements of machines...would have been farms and workshops.[239]

Greece and Rome lacked the entrepreneurial spirit and drive necessary to turn inventions and technological advancement into products and services that could benefit society at large. As a result, general welfare stagnated for centuries.

Entrepreneurship is not easy to grasp in an analytical way. The focus is on *productive* entrepreneurship, as opposed to what Baumol refers to as *redistributive* entrepreneurship. The latter can take a legal (lobbying for protection and other forms of rent seeking) or illegal (violence, bribery, fraud) form. Redistributive entrepreneurship, which is also sometimes referred to as "rent-seeking" behavior, is generally detrimental to the process of economic growth,[240] as one party or person's successes come at the expense of other parties or persons, with a tendency for overall welfare to suffer. Prevailing institutional arrangements largely determine which type of entrepreneurship will dominate.[241] The institutional arrangements that tend to favor productive entrepreneurship include democratic political organizations and those with well-established and well-protected rule of law.

Thus, productive entrepreneurship is a necessary condition to transform knowledge and human capital into products and services that improve society. Without substantial entrepreneurial input, turbochange can't happen, as Baumol, Litan, and Schramm noted: "Successful entrepreneurs economies *embrace* change and generally *encourage* change" [italics in original].[242]

Open competition is required for entrepreneurship to occur organically,[243] as competition is the lifeblood of an entrepreneurial, market-based economic system. When appropriately rewarded and stimulated, entrepreneurship constantly scans the expanding stock of knowledge and human capital, grasping and exploiting the most promising ideas and opportunities. The stimulating effect also works the other way around: the more successful entrepreneurship is in translating knowledge and human capital into profitable commercial applications, the more knowledge and human capital will stimulate the entrepreneurial machine. This is not to say that knowledge acquisition and human capital are driven only by a positive entrepreneurial environment, as other cultural, historical, and personal characteristics also influence their development.

The recognition of entrepreneurship as an absolutely crucial ingredient in the process of human advancement is relatively new. This is quite surprising, since, as William Baumol concluded in a thorough investigation of the history of entrepreneurship, "without [entrepreneurs], we would have basically nothing of the unprecedented growth miracle of the recent centuries."[244] Countless economic researchers explicitly recognize the contributions of entrepreneurs. Stanford University labor economist Edward Lazear, for example, wrote, "The entrepreneur is the single most important player in the modern economy."[245] In his landmark analysis of national economic advantage, Michael Porter of the Harvard Business School argued that entrepreneurship lies at its heart.[246]

Entrepreneurship is not valued in the world of economic research alone. Increasingly, political decision makers have begun to see the light. In 2002, Romano Prodi, then the president of the European Commission, made entrepreneurship the cornerstone of his economic strategy for the European Union: "Our lacunae in the field of entrepreneurship need to be taken seriously because there is mounting evidence that the key to economic growth and productivity improvements lies in the entrepreneurial capacity of an economy."[247] Prodi's implicit argument was that entrepreneurism's role in the process of economic growth had been systematically underestimated during the latter half of the 20th century by economists and policymakers alike. Prodi couldn't be more correct.

It's the Environment, Stupid

Despite all this high-mindedness about the importance of entrepreneurship, *The Economist's* 2013 argument still rings true: "Entrepreneurship is the modern-day philosopher's stone: a mysterious something that supposedly holds the secret to boosting growth and creating jobs."[248] It is even more striking to note that the entrepreneur is almost completely absent from the development of economic theory. Only in the "Austrian school" of economics does the entrepreneur occupy a consistently central role in the analysis,[249] as its adherent Schumpeter saw a crucial role for the entrepreneur in the process of economic development.[250] Gary Becker, one of the leading economists of the postwar period, humbly concluded, "As economists we have to admit that there was and is a major lacuna in our basic models. We omitted the entrepreneur from our models whereas it is more than obvious that entrepreneurs play an absolutely crucial role in the process of economic development."[251]

Before proceeding, I should qualify what I mean by "entrepreneurship." In a landmark study, the Organisation for Economic Co-operation and Development (OECD) defined entrepreneurs as

> agents of change and growth in a market economy… they can act to accelerate the generation, dissemination and application of innovative ideas…. Entrepreneurs not only seek out and identify potentially profitable economic opportunities but are also willing to take risks to see if their hunches are right.[252]

The legendary management guru Peter Drucker expressed the same basic idea: "Entrepreneurs innovate. Innovation is the specific instrument of entrepreneurship."[253] These definitions come close to identifying entrepreneurship as the result of a combination of the personal characteristics of its participants.[254] I call this the "DNA type" explanation of entrepreneurship.

If Society X has, for whatever reason, more men and women with DNA-type entrepreneurship than Society Y, that's bad news for Society Y. Society X will benefit from a thriving economy with increasingly better conditions for its inhabitants. This approach implies predestination depending on the distribution of certain personal characteristics.

Many specific theories have been developed in this realm, including that of sociologist Max Weber (1864–1920), who linked entrepreneurial drive and success to the Protestant work ethic.[255] Management professor Manfred Kets de Vries found that traumatic youth experiences often served as important motivational factors for entrepreneurs.[256] John Maynard Keynes (1883–1946) referred to "animal spirits" that served as "a spontaneous urge to action" among those with entrepreneurial drive.[257]

These explanations for the occurrence of entrepreneurship fall short of matching the historical record. For example, once the Berlin Wall fell, entrepreneurship exploded in formerly communist countries (of course, I admit that quite some of that flourishing entrepreneurship was of the crony-capitalism type). The DNA of the people involved, of course, hadn't changed. Instead, the environment in which those people conducted their daily business of life had completely changed. The "spontaneous urge to action" Keynes referred to was suddenly available, after decades of suppression under the old regimes. This change in the institutional environment turned thousands of men and women who were formerly obliged to pursue nonentrepreneurial ways of life into entrepreneurs—sometimes literally overnight. Unfortunately, the institutional characteristics of new systems and the lack of rule of law made purely redistributive, and even criminal, entrepreneurship quite rewarding in many of the former communist countries.

Thus, in order for an environment to stimulate productive entrepreneurship, it must feature the rule of law, the protection of property, a well-functioning banking and financial system, and a fiscal and regulatory framework conducive to entrepreneurial activity.[258] You must also consider how entrepreneurship is "embedded" in a particular society's culture and philosophy. The more deeply entrenched it is, the more intense it can become.[259]

Certain people are naturally inclined, via their personal characteristics (a drive to create wealth and success, a desire for independence, a nose for opportunities, religious conviction, a willingness to take risks, and so on), toward entrepreneurship. But they need positive reinforcement from society to act on those inclinations. As stated, a well-organized market economy has historically been best suited for Baumol's productive entrepreneurship,[260] but too often, people think of environments in which entrepreneurship thrives as being without rules. Nothing could be further from the truth. "Cowboy" or "casino" capitalism has no relationship to a well-functioning market economy interested in providing for its inhabitants. Instead, these economies have the *right kind* of rules and regulations.

Leftovers

In order to further explain the modern-day significance of entrepreneurship, I must explore the research and innovation process. So much knowledge is generated in a turbochange environment that not all the possible further ramifications and applications of it can, or will, be visible to those directly involved. This is certainly true for research activities within large corporations, which often complicate the way forward for new ideas with arduous decision making. Of course, most of the time, it's highly uncertain where most new ideas will lead. Leadership asks, *Does this new product or idea have the potential to become a major success? Or are its possibilities limited? Or nonexistent?* The decision-making hierarchies of large companies or research organizations often tend to be conservative about development of truly original ideas.

Within larger organizations, more focus is placed on incremental improvement in existing products and research programs. The financial risks involved in this approach are almost always smaller. As international political economy specialist Robert Gilpin recognized decades ago, firms that are technologically advanced tend to abandon innovative efforts in favor of "finding new markets for old products."[261]

To the same point, these organizations consider their heavy investments in existing technology and research programs and tend to favor increasing their return on them. Although CEOs of larger corporations often stress the need for daring innovation, their decision-making processes clearly favor initiatives in well-trod domains. The Harvard Business School's Clayton Christensen makes a clear distinction between sustaining technologies, or those that improve the performance of existing products, and disruptive technologies related to really new developments: He detects an "innovator's dilemma," the fact that the customer bases of most companies are not interested in disruptive technologies. Thus, companies that place greater focus on their existing customer base's needs tend to let disruptive technological innovations pass them by.[262]

In his book *The Free-Market Innovation Machine,* Baumol described a similar mechanism. He argued that established companies must fully engage in a continuing process of innovation. Therefore, most large corporations incorporated research and innovation into their core corporate strategies—with some inevitable consequences:

> The bureaucratic control of innovative activity in the large firm serves to ensure that the resulting changes will be modest, predictable and incremental. These firms are not predisposed to welcome the romantic flights of the imagination, the leaps of faith and plummets into the unknown that often lead only to disaster but which alone are likely to open up new worlds.[263]

A good example is the "resource revolution," the possibility to increase the productivity of natural resources by applying the latest innovations in information technology, biology, and nanotechnology. Forward-looking entrepreneurs are reaping the benefits of this revolution as established companies let the opportunities go by.[264]

In the 1950s, John Galbraith noted that "there is no more pleasant fiction than that technological change is the product of the matchless ingenuity of the small man forced by competition to employ his wits to better his neighbor." [265] Galbraith was both right and wrong. Technological discovery indeed takes place most often in large organizations. But Galbraith did not consider knowledge spillovers, which offer "the small man" enormous possibilities. As knowledge development intensifies, potential spillovers multiply. Baumol and his coauthors concluded:

> Radical breakthroughs tend to be disproportionally developed and brought to market by a single individual or new firm, although frequently, if not generally, the ideas behind the breakthrough originate in larger firms (or universities) that, because of their bureaucratic structures, do not exploit them. As Jean-Baptiste Say noted at the beginning of the nineteenth century, "without the entrepreneur (scientific) knowledge might possibly have lain dormant in the memory of one or two persons, or in the pages of literature."[266]

Thus, for benefits to flow throughout society, the conjoined twins human capital and entrepreneurship must continuously interact.

Picking Them Up
David Audretsch, Max Keilbach, and Erik Lehman of the Max Planck Institute of Economics have written about their "Knowledge Spillover Theory of Entrepreneurship."[267] The team defines entrepreneurship in this modern, turbochange-like context as

> the response to opportunities generated by investments in new knowledge made by incumbent firms and organizations, combined with their inability to fully and completely exhaust the ensuing opportunities to com-

mercialize that knowledge.... Entrepreneurship is the mechanism by which society more fully appropriates its investments in the creation of new knowledge, such as research and education.[268]

Of course, people are often entrepreneurial in traditional sectors of the economy, as well—perhaps creating a new type of café, launching new types of outlet stores, or developing new car or clothing designs—but this kind of entrepreneurship will not greatly affect the pace and intensity of turbochange. Technological development is *in itself* stimulating both entrepreneurial and intrapreneurial activity. As a group of researchers at General Electric put it:

> Open-source platforms and crowd-sourcing are quickly emerging as the most effective ways to unleash the creativity and entrepreneurship potential of the Global Brain. Individual companies are starting to gain expertise that extends well beyond their four walls, accessing a larger pool of talent which can vary depending on the problem at hand.[269]

Of course, the concept of entrepreneurship is incomplete without the factor of uncertainty. Entrepreneurs distinguish themselves by how they deal with the uncertainties of commercializing new knowledge. This emphasis has a long pedigree in the literature on economics and management.[270]

This view is in line with that of Daniel Isenberg, an entrepreneurial specialist teaching at Babson College and formerly at the Harvard Business School. Isenberg described entrepreneurs as "contrarian value creators,"[271] meaning that entrepreneurs see value where others don't. Integral to this sort of unique thinking is a readiness to deal with uncertainty. Some succeed, but many fail, inevitably. The successes attract attention, and the failures are usually quickly forgotten. But both successes and failures attract newcomers: Some plan to copy the success, and others are confident that they can do better.

These insights are in direct opposition to the late-20th-century perspective that in an increasingly knowledge-based economy, there would be *fewer* opportunities for smaller entrepreneurial actors. As Audretsch, Keilbach, and Lehman put it:

> Just as small and new firms confronted size-inherent scale disadvantages in the Solow economy, their inability to generate large investments in knowledge, at least in absolute terms, seemed to preclude them from developing a competitive advantage in the knowledge-based Romer economy.[272]

This view of limited entrepreneurial possibilities has been largely condemned to the dustbin of history. If more entrepreneurial drive is present, fewer, to paraphrase the late Mancur Olson, "big bills will be left on the sidewalk."[273] Entrepreneurs bring the ideas and inventions born out of the development of the stock of knowledge and human capital to real life. "Innovative entrepreneurs," Baumol and Strom concluded,

> create firms that offer new products, use new production processes, enter new markets, or adopt new forms of organization. The innovative entrepreneur's primary role is not invention. Rather, these individuals ensure the utilization of promising inventions by conceptualizing their best use and bringing them to the market.[274]

Given a relentlessly rising tide of knowledge and human capital, we can expect increasing opportunities for entrepreneurial activities that translate that new knowledge into real economic and social progress. Human capital and knowledge and entrepreneurship mutually reinforce one another.

For example, in the latter part of the 18th century, inventor James Watt and entrepreneur Matthew Boulton formed the firm Boulton & Watt in order to bring Watt's invention of the steam engine to the market.[275] By doing so, the two men almost singlehandedly started the first industrial revolution. Although the principles of the steam engine had already been understood and developed to some degree several times before in human history, it took the combination of a knowledge-inspired inventor (Watt) and an entrepreneur (Boulton) to bring the steam machine to market. Companies like Microsoft, Google, and Apple are modern examples of the extremely successful intermarriage of technology in human capital and entrepreneurial excellence.

Millennia Old, or Only Two Centuries?

So far I have discussed human capital and entrepreneurship, the first two elements of the earthly trinity that drives turbochange. I believe that an accelerating development of knowledge and intense entrepreneurial drive collude to create an environment that encourages multitudes of new products, services, modes of production and communication, and even completely new ways of thinking about and dealing with a bewildering variety of issues. In short, in such an environment, society changes at turbospeed.

Next, I'll turn to the third factor behind turbochange, globalization. The process of globalization intensifies and catalyzes the increasing returns to human capital, technology and knowledge, and entrepreneurship. Likewise, then, globalization also contributes to the instability and the many uncertainties and anxieties that come with turbochange.

Globalization has been defined in different ways. For example, economic historian David Landes defined globalization as

> a process that goes back centuries and varies in intensity with technological and social possibilities, the ups and

downs of business enterprise, the ever-changing uncertainties of war and peace. It is not a cause, not an ideology. It is simply the pursuit of wealth.[276]

Put another way, globalization is driven by the same human characteristics that create economic progress in a closed economy. Similarly, globalization has been described as "a widening, deepening, and speeding up of worldwide interconnectedness in all aspects of contemporary social life, from the cultural to the criminal, the financial to the spiritual."[277]

Economic historian Harold James defines globalization as "the integration of the world through large flows of goods, capital and people."[278] For the most part, *A Giant Reborn* hews close to James's definition. I believe that globalization is the integration of worldwide social, economic, and financial development through the flow of goods, capital, labor, knowledge, and technology. The addition of the last elements—knowledge and technology—is crucial to my argument. But certainly, some historical perspective is necessary to best understand the phenomenon of globalization.

Globalization's historical path has been hotly debated by economic historians, with three primary theories dominating the discussion. The first view takes a very long-term perspective, identifying forms of globalization all the way back to the fourth millennium BC. The German-born economic historian Andre Gunder Frank and his American colleague Jerry Bentley are well-known adherents of this view.[279] Bentley argued that well before 1500, "trade networks reached almost all regions of Eurasia and sub-Saharan Africa and large volumes of commerce encouraged specialization of agricultural and industrial production."[280] Those who share this view also cite the Roman Empire, pointing out that economic integration took place, at least to a certain extent, on an empire-wide scale.[281] Andre Gunder Frank and his coauthor Barry Wills took this idea further, claiming that "the existence of the same world system in which we live stretches back at least 5,000 years."[282]

The second theory sets the starting point of the history of globalization around 1500. Two years in particular are considered to be of extreme importance: 1492 and 1498. The first refers to the (re)discovery of the Americas by Columbus and the second to Vasco da Gama's successful journey around the African continent before his arrival in India. Adam Smith, the father of modern economic analysis, firmly believed that these two dates were among the most important in human history. Smith saw globalization as key to the development of an efficient and competitive economic system. *New York Times* columnist Thomas Friedman, a longtime student of globalization, is another disciple of this theory.[283]

But historians James Tracy, Kevon O'Rourke, and Jeffrey Williamson disagree, and their view forms the third theory. O'Rourke and Williamson concluded that because of a lack of movement among people and capital and a lack of convergence in the prices of worldwide available commodities, "globalization did not begin 5,000 years ago, or even 500 years ago. It began in the early nineteenth century."[284]

The Third Wave

According to this theory, however, globalization did not develop smoothly over the past two centuries. Instead, it came in three waves—two upward and one downward. O'Rourke and Williamson believe that the first wave started early in the nineteenth century and ended in the period 1870–1913. This first wave was mainly driven by important changes in both the possibilities and the cost of transportation; suddenly, there were, alongside the rise of the railroads, more reliable ships, a shift from sail to steam, the advent of the Suez and Panama Canals, and much better navigation tools. The intensification of international trade and massive international migration drove it even further. In the century before

1914, world trade grew by 5 percent on average per year—much higher than the overall economic growth of that century.

John Maynard Keynes, the most prominent economist of that era, described in his 1919 treatise *The Economic Consequences of the Peace* what the world had come to look like by the end of that first period of globalization:

> What an extraordinary episode in the economic prog-
> ress of man that age was which came to an end in
> August 1914!... The inhabitant of London could or-
> der by telephone, sipping his morning tea in bed, the
> various products of the whole earth, in such quantity
> as he might see fit, and reasonably expect their early
> delivery upon his doorstep; he could at the same mo-
> ment and by the same means adventure his wealth in
> the natural resources and new enterprises of any quar-
> ter of the world, and share, without exertion or even
> trouble, in their prospective fruits and advantages, or he
> could decide to couple the security of his fortunes with
> the good faith of the townspeople of any substantial
> municipality in any continent that fancy or informa-
> tion might recommend.... But, most important of all,
> he regarded this state of affairs as normal, certain, and
> permanent, except in the direction of further improve-
> ment, and any deviation from it as aberrant, scandalous
> and avoidable.[285]

Despite Keynes's prediction, globalization did indeed deviate from its path during the period 1914–1945, the downward cycle. Two world wars and the devastating Great Depression of the 1930s brought the process of worldwide integration to an end. For more than 30 years, deglobalization prevailed.

Abrupt reversal came about following World War II. The war's end in 1945 was the genesis of the third wave of modern globaliza-tion. Under the auspices of the United States, the Western world developed a market-based, open economic and trading system that allowed for massive improvements in quality of life and well-being, despite the pall cast by the Cold War.

During the 1970s and early 1980s, massive increases in oil prices caused several recessions and severely tested this new globalization-based international economic order. However, liberalization of economic activity in China and India, the fall of the Berlin Wall, and the implosion of the Soviet Union led globalization to shift into higher gear during the 1990s.

Extensive data perfectly illustrate globalization's intensity from the 1990s forward.[286] The McKinsey Global Institute's Worldwide Connectedness Index increased substantially between 1995 and 2012.[287] World exports, as a percentage of world gross domestic product (GDP), increased from around 18 percent in the early 1990s to above 30 percent by 2007 and 2008.

In 1990, trade in goods and services amounted to 16 percent of GDP in the rich OECD countries and 21 percent in emerging markets. By 2008, these numbers had risen to 29 percent and 37 percent, respectively. Cross-border capital flows increased from $1 trillion in 1990 to $11 trillion in 2007. World foreign direct investment as a percentage of world GDP stood at 1 percent in 1990, increased to more than 4 percent in 2000, dropped back to less than 2 percent in 2002–2004, and then climbed again to 3.5 percent in 2007.

The McKinsey Global Institute estimates that every year, 15 percent to 25 percent of world economic growth can be attributed to global flows of goods, services, and finance; in 2012, these reached $26 trillion. Cross-border flows of data and communication have exploded, expanding by more than 50 percent per year since 2005. The number of people with cellular phones rose from around 700 million in 2000 to more than 6 billion in 2012.[288] In 2000, fewer than 30 percent of these phone users were in emerging countries. By 2012, that share had risen to more than 75 percent.

Worldwide migration is also on the rise—but not at the heights it reached during the nineteenth century.

The financial crisis of 2008–2009 and the deep recession that followed it led to a pause, but not a halt, in globalization. *The Economist* concluded in late 2013 that "after two decades in which people, capital and goods were moving ever more freely across borders, walls have been going up, albeit ones with gates."[289] Whereas world exports as a percentage of world GDP had recovered by 2011 to 2008 levels, the recoveries of cross-border capital flows and foreign direct investment came about much more slowly.

The international integration of production networks and value chains quickly recovered from its limited dip during the years 2008–2009. "Increasing shares of the value of a product are added outside the region to which the country of completion belongs. 'Factory World' remains under construction, but this process is progressing at a fast pace," researchers focusing on global value chains concluded.[290]

Today, there can be no doubt that protectionist practices and inward-looking policymaking are on the rise. The financial and economic crises caused noticeable drops in corporate internationalization of R&D activities.[291]

On balance, however, chances that globalization will reverse are slim. Gideon Rachman of the *Financial Times* correctly noted that "it would certainly be morally dubious to attempt to bolster western living standards by undermining an economic trend that has dragged hundreds of millions of people out of poverty in the developing world."[292] The DHL Global Connectedness Index, which is compiled by Pankaj Ghemawat of New York University's Stern School of Business and Steven Altman of the IESE Business School, confirms that globalization is back on track following the difficult years during and immediately after the financial crisis. I tend to agree with *The Economist's* assertion that "the power of technology to erase distance is too strong, and the economic benefits of international trade and foreign investment are too strong."[293] The McKinsey Global Institute also concurs, arguing,

> two major forces are now accelerating the growth and evolution of global flows. The first is increasing global prosperity. By 2025, 1.8 billion people around the world will enter the consuming class.... Emerging-market consumers will spend $30 trillion annually, up from $12 trillion today.... The second major force is the growing pervasiveness of internet connectivity and the spread of digital technologies.[294]

These opinions from *The Economist* and the McKinsey Global Institute underscore the powerful forces that continue to push globalization forward, but it is a mistake to think that counterforces are not present as well. These counterforces are just as capable of using modern communication and marketing techniques to spread their arguments and mobilize troops. But even if globalization does slow for a longer period, it will remain a major catalyst for turbochange.

Standing on Adam's Shoulders

To better understand what globalization does to the process of economic growth, and hence to turbochange, I return to Adam Smith's arguments in *Wealth of Nations* (1776). According to Smith, the principal cause of economic growth is the division of labor, which leads to specialization and higher productivity. But Smith cautions that the possibility to arrive at a division of labor that is as efficient as possible is limited by what he describes as the "extent of the market." In fact, Chapter 3 of the first book of *Wealth of Nations* carries the title "That the Division of Labor Is Limited by the Extent of the Market" and opens with the following sentence: "As it is the power of exchanging that gives occasion to the division of labor, so the extent of this division must always be the extent of the power, or, in other words, by the extent of the market."[295]

Smith realized that a competitive internationalization of economic activity could boost the division of labor (specialization), leading to higher productivity and ultimately to greater income and wealth. He was dissatisfied with the British Empire for the very reason that it organized international trade in a monopolistic and uncompetitive way.

Of course, the "extent of the market" is constantly being broadened and deepened as Smith's division of labor has become an international phenomenon. As globalization progresses, more and more people get involved in the processes of consumption, production, investment, innovation, and research. As the incomes of these people grow, the process is reinforced. What Smith defined almost 250 years ago as the "power of exchanging" is strengthened each time globalization expands. As this happens, incentives sharpen for the development of human capital and knowledge and for entrepreneurial endeavors. Hence, globalization directly contributes to turbochange.

Globalization increases the extent of the market in several ways. First, as the world becomes more and more open, interactions leading to the development of human capital and new knowledge become more frequent. The McKinsey Global Institute has confirmed that globalization is intensifying this process, stating, "The knowledge-intensive portion of global flows increasingly dominates—and is growing faster than—capital- and labor-intensive flows."[296] The Institute estimates that in 2014, knowledge-intensive good flows grew 1.3 times faster than labor-intensive good flows.

Next, as more and more people and institutions get involved in research and development, they must begin to specialize or, to use Smith's terms, reinforce the division of labor. The increasing volume of knowledge renders limiting areas of further investigation unavoidable. Greater levels of specialization tend to increase the focus and efficiency of research and discovery processes and leads to new areas of interest.

At the same time, methods of communication have dramatically expanded, and those methods are also much faster than those of the past. As Joel Mokyr's access argument described, the communication revolution has tremendous impact on the extension of the market.

Globalization also helps enlarge the extent of the market via its impact on entrepreneurship. Since the Berlin Wall fell and the Chinese and Indian economies became much more liberal, the rate of entrepreneurship worldwide has exploded; nonparticipation in the entrepreneurial economy has become the exception, not the rule.[297] A quasi-worldwide spread of entrepreneurial drive has sharpened competition, intensifying the search for opportunities that can be profitably pursued. (Smith's dream has come true, so to speak.) As I outlined earlier, this intensified search process stimulates in its turn the further development of human capital, knowledge, and technological advancement.

Once again, the McKinsey Global Institute confirmed the massive impact of globalization on entrepreneurial activity worldwide:

> Companies, entrepreneurs and individuals have more opportunities to participate. Governments and multinational companies were once the only actors involved in cross-border exchanges, but today digital technologies enable even the smallest company or individual entrepreneur to be a "micromultinational" that sells and sources products, services, and ideas across borders. Traditional business models are being challenged by microscale activities ranging from microwork to micropayments and microshipments.[298]

As production and investment in developing (or emerging) economies grow, parts of the traditional production process in industrialized countries will shift. For example, consider textile and steel production. The major drivers of these industries—the assets its companies seek—are cheap labor and areas with less stringent regulation. First-movers among the emerging economies move up the ladder of the industrial added-value chain, and new entrants move in. As South Korea and Taiwan advanced, China supplanted them as the workshop of the world. Today, China faces increasing competition from nations like Vietnam and Bangladesh.

Innovation and technological advancement are imperative for the survival of companies in richer countries. Baumol wrote that in a free-market economy, firms are forced into "a continuing process of innovation, *because it becomes a matter of life and death for many of them.*"[299] Countries like the United States that lie on the frontier of knowledge development must intensify innovation in order to stay out in front.

Globalization also *in and of itself* contributes to the problems most societies encounter when trying to deal with turbochange. Its influence is at the root of the dynamics and structures of society and human interaction. Economic historian Michael Bordo wrote:

> Many fear globalization because of the changes it brings in the structure of national economies and a reduction in the living standards of some groups of society while others gain. They also resent the fact that decisions made in other countries impact their lives.[300]

Fellow economic historian Harold James added that globalization is inevitably also associated with "transfers of ideas and shifts of technology, which affect and restructure our preferences…. In consequence, globalization generates continuous uncertainty about values, both in [a] monetary and [a] more fundamental… sense."[301] James continued:

Some of the hardest obstacles to globalization are not
economic, but rather lie in the domain of social psychology. It is here that a sense of helplessness is profoundly pervasive. We find it hard psychologically to
deal with the consequences of global openness.[302]

Oceans of Instability and Uncertainty

So far, I've explored how turbochange is driven by rapid changes
in and the deepening of knowledge embodied in human capital
and the intensification of entrepreneurial drive, and that globalization accelerates these processes. The downside? The dynamics of
turbochange will not only be disturbing *in and of themselves* for
the economy and for society at large, but they will also fuel overall
instability. These disturbances influence the daily lives of people,
and worse yet, they create the threat of systemic risks. (Recall the
sudden fragility of the US economy in 2008.) I foresee three areas
where turbochange and its accompanying instability will cause the
greatest threat of systemic risks.

First on my agenda are the wealth consequences of the technological revolution we're currently witnessing—in particular, what
I refer to as the mounting real estate bias of modern societies. "In
an age of information and communication technology (ICT), it is
inevitable that we value what an ICT-intensive economy cannot
create," argued Adair Turner, the former chairman of the United Kingdom's Financial Services Authority and a member of the
British House of Lords.[303] According to some, the ICT revolution is still in its infancy, but it has already contributed greatly to
income inequality. Turner outlined some of the consequences of
this evolution:

> As the better off become richer...an increasing share
> of consumer expenditures is devoted to buying goods
> and services that are rich in fashion, design, and subjec-

tive brand values, and to competing for ownership of location-specific real estate. But if the land on which the desired houses and apartments sit is in limited supply, the inevitable consequence is rising prices.[304]

Rising values attract long- and short-term investors alike. As a consequence, Turner concluded, the economy may become

> inherently unstable because the more that wealth resides in real estate, the more the financial system will provide leverage to support real-estate speculation, which has been at the heart of all of the world's worst financial crises.[305]

As the financial crisis of 2008–2009 proved beyond any doubt, speculative over investment in real estate is a recipe for disaster. The crises that result from this speculation are detrimental to the welfare and well-being of large segments of the population, causing negative effects like increased instability and uncertainty in the real economy of investment, value creation, and jobs. Regulatory and monetary policies must be fundamentally changed in order to counteract the real estate bias.

Turbochange also increases systemic risk due to the consequences of increased integration.[306] Previously, I elaborated on globalization's role as a catalyst for turbochange. It produces a more integrated world in terms of flows of goods, services, capital, people, technology, and knowledge. When reviewing the research on integrated networks, Andrew Haldane, chief economist at the Bank of England and a keen observer of the modern social, economic, and financial environment, found that such networks tend to be simultaneously

> stable and unstable, calm and turbulent, robust-yet-fragile. They sit atop a cliff-edge, on one side of which are the sunny uplands of stability, on the other the stormy lowlands of fragility. The more connected and integrated the system, the more precipitate this cliff-edge.[307]

This situation is becoming more and more visible in physical (computer systems), social (epidemics), and economic (financial systems) networks alike. The financial crisis of 2008–2009 offers a virtually perfect example of how conditions that appeared to be calm and comfortable turned quickly and abruptly into the perfect storm. Risk overwhelmed, and almost destroyed, the system.

Modern society can increasingly be characterized as consisting of "complex adaptive systems" that generally perform in "highly efficient way [but] sometimes break down catastrophically."[308] William White, a senior advisor at the OECD and the former chief economist at the Bank for International Settlements, defined complex adaptive systems as sharing at least four basic properties: "(1) the inevitability of crises...(2) the impossibility of forecasting, (3) the absence of any relationship between the trigger for a systemic breakdown and its size, and (4) the inevitability of unforeseen consequences of all policy actions."[309] Turbochange will dramatically increase the number of these complex adaptive systems. As technology and knowledge advance, so too will integration, making the "cliff-edge" characteristic more pronounced. This situation will unavoidably lead to more instability and uncertainty.

The third factor that contributes to increased instability and uncertainty is information abundance. The Internet and social media like Twitter and Facebook provide instant information. Commerce sites like eBay and Amazon allow trade on the spot. In these areas, new developments take place much faster than books and magazines about them can be published. What is revolutionary today will likely be outdated tomorrow. More than 40 years ago, Herbert Simon, who won the Nobel Prize in Economics in 1978 for his research on the decision-making process in organizations, wrote:

> In an information-rich world, the wealth of information means a dearth of something else: a scarcity of what-

ever it is that information consumes. What information consumes is rather obvious: it consumes the attention of recipients. Hence a wealth of information creates a poverty of attention.[310]

This attention deficit is bound to reduce the quality of decision making and to place too much focus on short-term issues.

Haldane concluded that in these circumstances, the prospect becomes

a myopia trap. For addicts, shortened horizons generate a quest for quick fixes which further shorten horizons in a downward spiral. For gamblers, a sequence of losses shortens horizons and increases risk-taking. For depression sufferers, low confidence in the future become self-fulfilling.[311]

In conclusion, systemic risks increase in an environment of information overabundance, despite the perception that access to more information might improve decision-making abilities—not least because it allows for continual reappraisal of decisions. Instead, the information problem tends to fuel instability and uncertainty.

A Dizzying Velocity

Clearly, the world in which we live is at a significant turning point. Turbochange, the change process in overdrive, is afoot. The driving forces behind the process of turbochange—technological advancement, the development of human capital and knowledge, and entrepreneurship—are further strengthened and intensified by globalization.

Eric Brynjolfsson and Andrew McAfee of MIT's Center for Digital Business described "the second machine age" that followed the Industrial Revolution as "forever transform[ing] how physical work was done." Brynjolfsson and McAfee's second machine age had three outstanding features:

> Sustained exponential improvement in most aspects of computing, extraordinarily large amounts of digitized information, and recombinant innovation. These three forces are yielding breakthroughs that convert science fiction into everyday reality, outstripping even our recent expectations and theories. What's more, there's no end in sight.... How can we be so sure? Because the exponential, digital, and recombinant powers of the second machine age have made it possible for humanity to create two of the most important one-time events in our history: the emergence of real, useful, artificial intelligence (AI) and the connection of most of the people on the planet via a common digital network.[312]

Turbochange will bring progress, advancement, benefits to public welfare, and an escape from poverty for millions around the world. At the same time, it will also inevitably bring about "an age of continual discontinuity[313] that causes uncertainty and instability, including systemic turbulence. In imagining such a future, and speaking of turbochange as a kind of "sonic boom," Gregg Easterbrook wrote,

> Many problems that have characterized recent decades are likely to get worse.... Job instability, economic insecurity, a sense of turmoil, the unfocused fear that even when things seem good a hammer is about to fall.... While envisioning the likelihood of a global boom, [I] also warn that when it comes to anxiety, you ain't seen nothing yet.... The velocity of change could become dizzying.... Every little thing that goes wrong anywhere in the world will scare us. And we will know every little thing that goes wrong anywhere in the world.[314]

This increased uncertainty and instability will make turbo-change a demanding process. Not every society or community will be able to deal with it in a positive and efficient way. To make matters worse, turbochange will likely destabilize some societies. Brynjolfsson and McAfee warned,

> Technological progress is going to leave behind some people, perhaps even a lot of people.... There's never been a better time to be a worker with special skills or the right education.... However, there's never been a worse time to be a worker with only "ordinary" skills and abilities to offer.[315]

As the winds of turbochange gather strength, skill-biased technological change will move to the forefront.[316] A winner-take-all society may prevail.[317] Societies with lower-skilled workforces will face structural unemployment, and income inequality will rise. Turbochange will likely bring about massive backlashes in some societies from time to time.

So, societies and countries that can adapt best to turbochange's demanding circumstances will take the lead—economically, politically, and militarily speaking. Their economies will develop much more quickly than others. Their productivity levels will soar. They will project power, prestige, and influence.

I believe that the United States is the country best equipped to deal with the challenges posed by turbochange. In Chapter 3, I will substantiate that claim via an analysis deeply rooted in economics, corporate strategies, institutional arrangements, and politics that also explores historical roots, social norms, and ingrained attitudes in the United States.

Chapter 3

The Restless Nation

THE STORY OF AMERICAN DECLINE, I'VE ARGUED, SEEMS unshakeable. Practically since its birth, people have been predicting the imminent downfall of the United States and its people. Each phase of declinism was accompanied by claims that this time around, America's downfall was *really* for real. Although the United States survived extremely difficult periods like the Civil War, the Great Depression, the Vietnam War, the 9/11 terrorist attacks, and the mother of all financial crises in 2008–2009, time and again, the doomsayers have been proven wrong. No matter how enormous the challenges are, one way or another, Americans always fight back and keep scrambling for the top. Always, that is, until now.

Does America's historical resilience offer any guarantee of domination in the 21st century and beyond? Is that chapter in world history coming close to its end here and now, or is there still more to be written? And of course, the big question: If America's preeminence will endure, as I argue, what factors will underpin this continuity, given a background of turbochange? How is the United States different from former hegemonic powers, such as the Habsburg, French, or British Empires? What is so special about the United States that allows it to break the "succession of hegemonies" that have prevailed in world politics?[318]

But first: Isn't it already too late? Hasn't the Rubicon already been crossed? This time, isn't the decline irreversible? According to some analysts, yes. For example, Arvind Subramanian, the former International Monetary Fund (IMF) researcher and advisor to the Indian government, doubled down about America's demise as *the* superpower by writing an article entitled, "The Inevitable Superpower: Why China's Rise Is a Sure Thing."[319]

Yesterday's Power?

During the 1950s, the general consensus among leading academic economists (including MIT's Paul Samuelson) was that the Soviet Union was bearing down on the United States in terms of economic capabilities and power. Naturally, most believed this would also have a major impact on the comparative military capabilities of the West and the Soviet bloc; in fact, then-chief of the CIA Allen Dulles was quite explicit about the prospect of fading American dominance.[320]

But from the mid-1960s onward, it dawned on economists and intelligence analysts that the Soviet Union's surge forward was stalling out.[321] The rest of the story is, of course, history. The rise and fall of the Soviet economy and empire has several unique aspects, but this historical episode holds an important lesson for 21st-century reflections on similar issues. It is always somewhat reckless, and most of the time wrong, to think in a linear way about future developments by comparing them to things that took place in the recent past. Usually, the future is *not* a linear continuation of past decades.

As the idea of Soviet dominance has been relegated to the dustbin of history, China is now the focus. Since the publication of a famous 2003 article by economists at the investment bank

Goldman Sachs on the concept of BRIC, a cabal of developing economies,[322] an industry has developed around the question of exactly when China would overtake the United States as the largest economy of the world. Name any year between 2015 and 2050, and it has been put forward as *the* year. Acceptance of the idea that China will eclipse the United States as an economic, political, and military power seems almost universal; literally hundreds of books have been written on the subject.[323]

Of course, economic supremacy carries important consequences for military relations and for the world order, whatever it might be. The declinist view places Washington in second or even third place with respect to worldwide political and military influence. In addition to China, the European Union, India, Russia, and Brazil are pushing the United States further down the ladder of world power, according to some analysts and pundits. Other countries— Turkey, Indonesia, and Mexico, for example—are knocking on the door too. The "Rise of the Rest," as described by Alice Amsden, seems to become more real every day.[324]

But is this premise warranted? GDP is the most commonly used indicator of an economy's size,[325] and GDP per capita is used to measure the individual well-being of a society's citizens.[326] When considering GDP and GDP per capita, distinction must be made between measurement in currencies (specifically, the US dollar) and measurement in terms of purchasing power parity (PPP). In a PPP approach, you compare what $1 US buys in the United States with what that same dollar buys in other countries. Of course, the purchasing power of $1 US in China buys much more than $1 in the United States or, for that matter, in any other advanced economy, like Japan, Germany, or Australia.

Hence, PPP adjustments tend to enlarge the economic size of emerging markets versus the more advanced economies. The main reason: In an emerging economy, labor and land tend to

be much cheaper than those resources are in advanced economies. In emerging countries, a significant portion of consumers'
expenditures are made on locally produced goods. Labor services
also tend to be much cheaper in poorer countries because they
have lower overall productivity.[327] As economies mature, these PPP
differences tend to level off.

In terms of GDP as measured in PPP, China is catching up
with America.[328] According to the database of the IMF, at the
end of 2013 the United States represented 16.4 percent of the
world economy, and China represented 15.8 percent. However, PPP data offer too simplistic an image of what is really happening in these economies and their relative positions in the
world order.

Not so Fast

When comparing living standards, PPP-adjusted data like GDP
per capita tend to better reflect differences among countries. If,
however, you are more interested in the relative importance of
countries in terms of economic and geopolitical weight, it is more
instructive to look at data in terms of the dominant world currency. The price of and trade in high-technology products, factors of production like oil and other raw materials, licensing and
related agreements, and advanced services are most important
in this respect. It's also worth noting that foreign investments
and major international financial transactions take place in the
most easily and transparently available currency. Most of the time,
that currency is the US dollar. Thus, when measuring the relative
economic and geopolitical weight of countries, it's best to consider
the data in US dollars.

The latest data on GDP in US dollars as compiled by
the World Bank is from 2013; it ranks the largest economies
(in billions):

United States	$16.768
China	$9.240
Japan	$4.920
Germany	$3.730
France	$2.806
UK	$2.679
Brazil	$2.246
Italy	$2.150
Russia	$2.097
India	$1.877

When measured in US dollars, the US economy is still 80 percent larger than the Chinese economy. The Chinese, Japanese, and German economies *combined* are just slightly larger than the US economy. Counting from the bottom of the chart, you would have to combine the Indian, Russian, Italian, Brazilian, British, French, and German economies to create an entity comparable to the US economy. The 19 European countries that use the euro have a combined GDP of $13.134 billion—more than 20 percent smaller than the American economy; the 28 countries that make up the EU have a combined GDP a bit larger than the United States. Clearly, the American economy is still in a league of its own.

As I mentioned earlier, GDP per capita is the best indicator of the well-being of a country's citizens. Between the United States and China, even larger differences show up in GDP per capita than in overall GDP. At the end of 2013, GDP per capita measured in $ US stood in the United States at $53,042, and in China, $6,807—a difference of close to 8 to 1. That means that China's GDP per capita is just above Peru's and slightly under…Iraq's.

Adjusted for PPP, the difference closes up to 5 to 1: $53,001 for the United States, $11,868 for China. In the IMF's rank of PPP-adjusted GDP per capita nations, China is in 89th place, with the Dominican Republic and the Maldives just above it and Jordan and Peru just below it.

By the way, in 2013, the IMF listing for PPP-adjusted GDP per capita ranks the United States in tenth place, with $53,001. In the top position is Qatar ($145,894), followed by Luxembourg ($90,833) and Singapore ($78,762). The other countries that rank ahead of the United States are Brunei, Kuwait, Norway, United Arab Emirates, San Marino, and Switzerland—not surprisingly, all small countries that have either at least one extremely well-developed sector or one abundantly available prime resource (banking, oil, etc.). Among the larger economies of the world, Australia is closest to the United States with a PPP-adjusted GDP per capita 15 percent smaller than the American one. Next in line are Germany and Canada (both at –18 percent) with Japan 30 percent behind the United States. If you index the PPP-adjusted GDP per capita of the United States in 2013 at 100, Russia indexes at 46, Brazil at 28, China at 22, and India at 10.

Gaps—or Canyons?

Clearly, an enormous gap still exists between the United States and China in terms of GDP per capita as well as in overall economic size. The obvious next questions: Whether, how, and/or when can China bridge those gaps?

So let's do the math, first for the overall economy. In rounded numbers, the US economy is valued at $16.8 trillion and the Chinese economy at $9.2 trillion. If the US economy grows at 3 percent and the Chinese at 7 percent, the US GDP would expand by $504 billion in the first year, and the Chinese GDP would expand by $644 billion. China is closing the gap in this scenario, no doubt. But in 2013 dollars and assuming all the other relevant circumstances as constant, it would take China 54 years to catch up with the United States in terms of overall GDP.[329] "China is rising," concluded Michael Beckley, a political scientist at Tufts University, "but it is not catching up."[330]

That 7 percent growth figure may seem quite modest, given Chinese economic performance over the last three decades, but there are indications that such an annual growth figure might not be easily attainable in the future. Harvard economists Lant Pritchett and Larry Summers have written of the idea of "regression to the mean" as the most salient feature of the history of economic growth.[331] Extensive historical research has shown that abnormally rapid economic growth never persists in the long run. Growth can continue at an impressive pace for a considerable period of time if the starting point is very low—as was clearly the case with China.[332] When Deng Xiaoping began reforming China in the late 1970s, it was among the poorest and, economically speaking, least developed countries in the world. China benefited strongly from what Alexander Gerschenkron first labeled as the advantage of "economic backwardness."[333]

Further analysis by Pritchett and Summers has shown that in emerging countries, periods of rapid growth are frequently followed by sudden drop-offs, turning points that are as unexpected as they are drastic. China experienced 35 years of remarkably high economic growth; given such factors as its high levels of state control and corruption and the repressive nature of its political regime, Pritchett and Summers advise forecasters, planners, and analysts to look at a much wider range of outcomes for future Chinese economic growth than just an extrapolation of the trends of those past 35 years. Josef Joffe is a little more explicit here: "As the baseline goes higher, as economies mature, growth slows. This is a law of economic history that even China and India cannot endlessly defy."[334]

Many claim that Asia, and China in particular, have very different economic models, but I find no reason to assume that nations on the Asian continent are different in terms of growth dynamics. Japan has provided ample evidence that growth can stall for very long periods of time: it grew impressively during the 1960s and 1970s, got stuck by the end of the 1980s, and has been in quasi-continuous trouble since the 1990s. Research by Pritchett and Summers has made a strong case for the idea that growth in China will begin to obey the law of regression to the mean as well, with high-speed growth starting to level off after about 30 years. Josef Joffe has argued that we should not be confusing "the natural, soaring flight at the beginning with long-range aviation.... You can't invest 50 percent of GDP and then expect each increment of investment is going to yield more."[335]

It is much safer to assume that in the future, China will see growth rates of around 3 to 4 percent annually. If we go with the 4 percent growth rate, China will add $368 billion to its GDP—clearly less than the $504 billion the United States would add at a 3 percent growth rate. If American growth slows to 2 percent, its GDP would grow by $336 billion, marginally less than the $368 billion attributed to China. In this latter case, it would take China 238 years to catch up with the United States in terms of overall dollar-denominated GDP.[336]

Things look even more challenging for China when analyzing the data by GDP per capita. As I stated earlier, it makes more sense to examine PPP-adjusted data when comparing standards of living between countries. At the end of 2013, PPP-adjusted GDP per capita stood at $53,001 for the United States and $11,868 for China, a gap of $41,133. Suppose America's GDP per capita grows by 1 percent annually (or, in 2013 dollar terms, by $530 per year), and the Chinese GDP per capita grows by 4.5 percent annually (which would be truly extraordinary, since a similar increase in labor productivity must happen in order for that to take place). That would mean that Chinese GDP per capita would increase by, say, $530 per year. Thus, China's GDP per capita would have to grow by 4.5 percent to the United States' 1 percent in order to *not* increase the *nominal* gap in GDP per capita. If China falls below that 4.5 percent level, the nominal gap between US GDP per capita and Chinese GDP per capita *widens*.

Of course, the *relative* gap between US and Chinese GDP per capita declines if China succeeds in holding the nominal gap constant. If you use data from 2013, US GDP per capita is 4.47 times the Chinese GDP per capita. If both countries' GDP per capita increases by, say, $30,000, the US's GDP per capita would be 1.98 times China's GDP per capita.[337] The conclusion seems straightforward.

Certainly, China will, one way or the other, play an important role in world politics in the future. But I argue that the prospect of China as an inevitable superpower is far from certain. In terms of overall GDP as measured in dollar terms, China will probably be able to catch up with the United States, but it will take much more time than most assume; in fact, there's no way it will happen in the 21st century. Barring apocalyptic scenarios for the United States, it is hard for me to see how China can ever catch up. A World Bank analysis concluded that up to 80 percent of the wealth of the United States is composed of intangible assets, such as the country's system of property rights; its independent judicial system; and the knowledge, skills, and trust that are core to American society.[338] China is a long way behind, to say the very least.

Turbostress

Despite all the declinist rhetoric to the contrary, the United States is still the leading economic, political, and military power in the world. The world is on its way to—and, to some extent, already in the midst of—a period of turbochange, with ever more rapid changes in technology, social and economic conditions, and the environment and society at large. Human capital and knowledge have led to new insights in all sciences, both basic and applied. Entrepreneurship has intensified throughout the world since the fall of the Berlin Wall in 1989, leading to an overwhelming flow of new ideas, technologies, business ventures, lifestyles, products, and services. The phenomenon of globalization, the third driving force behind turbochange, has amplified these effects.

As a consequence, modern society must constantly adjust and renew. As the intensity of this pressure grows, potential for destabilizing forces rises for countless reasons, including factional infighting among different interest groups as they compete to preserve their respective advantageous positions. Thus, turbochange also tends to produce turbostress within a society, posing a threat to its stability.

Turbostress is also a factor when it comes to political policy. As Gregg Easterbrook correctly noted, "there will be tremendous pressure on government officials and policymakers to do something, anything, about the sense of accelerating change.... But stop change? All the air, naval, and ground forces in the world could not accomplish that."[339] Policymakers will find it increasingly difficult to cope with all this societal change in a constructive manner. Thus, they'll tend to play it safe, as safeguarding the status quo will be seen as the least disturbing option. That is, however, rarely the optimal choice in an environment experiencing turbochange. Societies that are poorly equipped to deal with the consequences of turbochange will inevitably fall behind.

Although the declinists believe that the United States is already in a death spiral, I conclude that the reverse will prove to be true, as the United States is best equipped to deal in a constructive and productive way with the societal stresses of turbochange. Its culture and economy will be more attractive to researchers and entrepreneurs. A virtuous cycle will ensue.

Trouble at the Bottom

If the United States is to maintain dominance in human capital, it must educate its citizens well. John Nye, a professor of political science at Harvard University who served as assistant secretary of defense during the Clinton administration, summarized the state of affairs (as he saw it) in American education:

> American education at its best—many universities and the top slice of the secondary education system—meets or sets the global standard. But American education at its worst—too many primary and secondary schools, especially in less affluent districts—lags badly behind. This means that the quality of the labor force will not keep up with the rising standards needed in an information-driven economy.... Improvement in the country's K-12 education system will be necessary if the country is to meet the standards needed in an information-based economy.[340]

Nye's argument: Top at the top, bad and getting worse at the bottom. The media is full of similar accounts. Some research backs up this negative read on the K-12 system; for example, an international comparison of the performance and abilities of 15- and 16-year-olds by the OECD revealed that US students were *not* among the top performers in mathematics, reading, and sciences.[341] However, if the OECD's data are corrected for demographic differences and differences in migration flows, the results are substantially different. After making such adjustments, Tino Sanandaji of Stockholm's Research Institute of Industrial Economics concluded that "American students outperform Europe by significant margins and tie with Asian students."[342] Stefan Halper, senior fellow at Cambridge University's Centre for International Studies, concurred:

> Comparing US and Danish education achievement, for example, compares a small, homogenous country, focused on its quality of life—and a large, diverse, global leader, home to a million legal immigrants since 2000

and an unknown number of illegals, the majority of
whom are impoverished and do not speak English.[343]

The conclusion seems to be that US students' overall scores
are lagging because of an influx of immigrants who lack facility
with the predominant language. (Yet this influx is, I believe, highly
beneficial to American society in several respects, which I'll cover
later.) Also, research has shown that skill gaps and shortages are not
any more pronounced in the United States than in other industrialized countries.[344] My opinion is that the US educational system
is at the top already, but there is of course substantial room for
improvement. Such improvement will be necessary in an environment of turbochange.

The dominance of two teacher's unions—the American Fed-
eration of Teachers (AFT) and the National Education Association (NEA)—over the US K-12 educational system seems to be
the cause of many of its structural problems. Their monopolistic
power has led to lifetime job security for teachers, pay scales based
on seniority instead of performance, early retirement, long holi-
days—the list goes on. The late Albert Shanker, a former president
of the AFT, once pointedly said: "When schoolchildren start paying union dues that's when I'll start representing the interests of
schoolchildren."[345] Teachers often lack motivation and innovation,
and their high pay and expensive benefits stretch the schools' bud-
gets. Hiring better teachers improves educational outcomes, but
the unions' power makes this difficult.[346]

Joel Klein served for many years as the chancellor of the New
York City Department of Education, the largest K-12 public
school system in the United States. He complained bitterly about
the "institutional stranglehold of defenders of the status quo."[347]
Political scientist James Kurth of Swarthmore College concluded:
"Numerous attempts to reform the monopolistic public schools
have failed; the solution will come by enabling a large variety of

private schools to freely compete with government ones."[348] I agree that the lack of innovation in US schools has much to do with the public monopoly. More competition seems to lead to remarkable improvements in educational outcomes.[349]

Top at the Top

At the university level, however, the United States is clearly at the top. The Center for World-Class Universities at Shanghai Jiao Tong University in China ranks the top universities in the world; in 2014, it found that 17 out of the top 20 world-class universities were American, with Harvard, Stanford, and MIT topping the list. The highest-ranked non-American university cracks the list at number nine.[350]

Research universities like MIT, Stanford University, and the University of Chicago are largely responsible for this dominance in the development of human capital and knowledge. The idea of founding universities focused on research began in Prussia in the early 19th century. (Berlin's Humboldt University was a pioneer.) The concept of research universities came to United States shortly after the end of the Civil War, but initially successes were limited.[351] After World War II, however, these research universities became "the core of the US science and technology system."[352]

Scientist Vannevar Bush (no relation to Presidents George H.W. and George W.) published a groundbreaking report immediately after World War II that focused on the need for research and made the case for this research to deal with investigation as well as with practical applications. Bush suggested that the government substantially expand its support of scientific research, and subsequent administrations implemented his call to action. The National Science Foundation was established in 1950. "Other countries," researchers Atkinson and Blanpied concluded, "have tried to replicate the success of US research universities, but with limited results."[353]

Israeli historian and education specialist Itamar Rabinovich characterized the superiority of the US higher education system as having to do with

> the traditional idea of the university as an institution that, beyond the teaching, research, and the transmission of knowledge, plays a unique role in generating fresh ideas, educating young people to think independently and critically, and preserving and extending the traditional body of cultural heritage...in the end it is the autonomy, scope of private governance and widespread social devotion to both philanthropy and well-financed higher education in the United States that ensures the global superiority of its institutions of higher learning, and these are cultural characteristics that other countries will be hard-pressed to replicate.[345]

Top American universities unashamedly pursue the most gifted students and try to bring out the best in these top students, inevitably at the expense of less-gifted ones. This policy is in sharp contrast to the practice at most European universities, which stress equality over excellence. Many Asian universities stress conformity to the norm instead of independent inquiry and criticism of accepted truths.[355] If creativity, inventiveness, and flexibility are qualities that are crucial to success in an environment of turbochange, equality and conformity are not the best characteristics to encourage. Education and enlightenment also play crucial roles in supporting respect for democratic institutions, just as ignorance protects despots.[356]

The Advantage of Having Less Past

I now turn to entrepreneurship, the second major driver of turbochange. Economic historian Louis Cain of Loyola University noted that what became the United States of America was born of entrepreneurship.[357] What is today the United States did indeed come into existence as an entrepreneurial initiative. In 1607 the Virginia Company, chartered by the British King James I,[358] sent three ships overseas with the purpose of setting up settlements on the coast of North America.[359] The passengers who stepped on shore in what would become Jamestown, Virginia, went mainly into the business of establishing plantations. Soon enough these first settlers saw themselves confronted with the possibility of failure—that not-so-pleasant but integral part of entrepreneurship—because some of their first ventures went badly wrong. Only after one John Rolfe introduced West Indian tobacco as an alternative crop did Virginian entrepreneurship start to pay off. The Virginia Company, however, went bust. It is certainly also true that many of the early settlements in New England were religiously inspired but, as historian John Steele Gordon concluded, "even in the theocracy that was early New England, the entrepreneurial spirit burned bright."[360]

It's tempting to agree. There's no denying that entrepreneurship is deeply ingrained in American society. In the midst of the mother of all financial crises, *The Economist* expressed it unequivocally: "Despite all its current woes, America remains a beacon of entrepreneurialism."[361] The British weekly went on to describe the rich history of entrepreneurship in America:

> It was founded and then settled by innovators and risk-takers who were willing to sacrifice old certainties for new opportunities. American schoolchildren are raised on stories about inventors such as Benjamin Franklin and Thomas Edison. Entrepreneurs such as Andrew Carnegie and Henry Ford are celebrated in monuments all over the place.... If anything, America's infatuation with entrepreneurialism has deepened further of late.

The information and communication technology (ICT) revolution alone has created a litany of American entrepreneurial celebrities like the late Steve Jobs, Bill Gates, Larry Page, and Mark Zuckerberg.

Entrepreneurship's entrenchment in American culture has much to do, believes economic historian Joel Mokyr of Northwestern University, with the adventurous spirit and openness to risk taking common among those who ventured to strike out to the British colonies. In a more general analysis of the links between technological creativity and economic progress, Mokyr wrote that "political and mental diversity combined to create an ever-changing panorama of technologically creative societies"; this undoubtedly holds true for the United States.[362]

But there's more to the story than just a collection of risk takers looking for prosperity and happiness in a faraway country. Crucial to the development of the entrepreneurial spirit was the fact that

> America did not have the burden of hundreds of years of economic cronyism. There were no aristocrats, no guilds, no ancient monopolies, or hereditary tariffs as there were in continental Europe.... We had less past than any other country, and therefore we *could* make our own history, creating the most Smithian economy in the western world.[363]

In this passage, John Steele Gordon's mention of the "Smithian economy" refers to the economic system characterized by free initiative, competitive forces, and open markets coherently described for the first time by Adam Smith in his 1776 book *Wealth of Nations*. Steele Gordon adds: "The US has consistently come closer to the Smithian ideal, over a longer period of time, than any other major nation."[364]

Needless to say, Smithian economic systems don't just fall out of the sky. As Daron Acemoglu and James Robinson illustrated in their magnum opus *Why Nations Fail,* productive economic systems only come about when the political decision-making process creates the institutions that are necessary to achieve them.[365] Naomi Lamoreaux, a professor of economic history at Yale University, summarized the early evolution in the newly created United States as follows:

> The Constitution facilitated entrepreneurship by creating the largest free-trade zone in the world, by prohibiting state governments from abrogating contracts or tampering with the value of money, and by giving the federal government the authority to create a system of intellectual property rights.[366]

Lamoreaux is correct: The Constitution ratified in June 1788 contained clauses on the sanctity of contracts, the protection of property rights, and a prohibition on restrictions on interstate commerce. The creation of patent law was also key to the growth of entrepreneurial activity. As historian Steven Lubar of Brown University concluded: "Nineteenth-century patent law embodied a delicate balance of monopoly, to encourage invention; the dissemination of new ideas, to encourage the increase of knowledge; and ease of use of patents, to encourage innovation."[367] I'll return to these issues later in this chapter.[368]

The Diversity Dividend

Another critical element of the entrepreneurial-friendly environment was the financial system created by Alexander Hamilton, the country's first secretary of the Treasury. In the words of economic historian Richard Sylla of New York University, Hamilton's system "helped to institutionalize entrepreneurship."[369] Its constant availability of (cheap) money to finance entrepreneurial initiatives further stimulated the climate.

Many are quick to claim that this cheap money has also contributed to the bubbles and financial crises the country regularly
experiences. While this seems accurate upon first consideration,
there's more to it than meets the eye. Radical innovation pushed by
the entrepreneurial class seems to go hand in hand with the boom-
and-bust nature of financial markets.[370] The dynamics of this process are well known. A new technology pops up—automobiles,
computers, the Internet—and thousands of entrepreneurs take a
shot at it. Investors place their bets on several competitors in an attempt not to miss the ultimate winner. The story always ends with
a few winners and many losers. In short, if the goal is a truly innovative and entrepreneurial economy, you must accept frequent
financial crises. Thus, the regularity with which booms and busts
have occurred during American history shows more strength than
weakness—no matter how much damage is done in the short run.

Entrepreneurship in America is also bolstered by the culture's
early and enduring acceptance of failure. John Steele Gordon argued that "while bankruptcy in Europe has always been regarded as moral as well as financial failure, this has not been the case
here—possibly because we are descendants of people who sought
a second chance by immigrating."[371] More than anywhere else,
in the United States success and failure are accepted as two sides
of the same coin. In his investigation of the transatlantic growth
gap that has occurred in the post–Great Recession period, Daniel
Gros of the Centre for European Policy Studies (CEPS) concluded
that the differences in bankruptcy procedures between the United
States and Europe have played a significant role. The American
system, so Gros concludes, is better in terms of economic recovery
because "losses can be recognized more quickly and over-indebted
households can start afresh, without being shackled for years."[372]

By and large, the entrepreneurship-positive system Hamilton created has remained intact over the last two centuries. There
have been ups and downs, of course, but entrepreneurship has

remained a core value. Immigrants eager to improve their destinies have always streamed vigor into this entrepreneurial climate, and they likely always will.[373] The US's relatively inclusive and tolerant approach allows it to profit from the "diversity dividend" that immigration invariably brings to entrepreneurship and economic development.[374]

Entrepreneurialism has become part of America's culture and identity, much more so than in most European countries. For example, the United States continuously scores high in the World Bank's annual ranking of countries' ease of doing business. In the 2013 ranking, the United States ranked fourth, behind Singapore, Hong Kong, and New Zealand.

Other rankings and studies on entrepreneurialism and ease of doing business, such as the Global Entrepreneurship Monitor and the World Economic Forum's yearly report on global economic competitiveness, consistently rate the United States among the best. Joseph Nye concluded that the United States is still "ahead of other countries in opportunities for entrepreneurship because it has a favorable business culture, the most mature venture capital industry, close relations between universities and industry, and an open immigration policy."[375] Even among Asian entrepreneurs, the United States has tremendous pull.[376]

The Reluctant Internationalist

So if turbochange requires a culture replete with development of human capital and knowledge on one hand and entrepreneurial drive and success on the other, I've proven that the United States is in a good place on both accounts. But what of globalization, the third driving force behind turbochange? Any globalization discussion must focus on the society's attitudes toward free trade, free movement of people, and openness to international investment. Does the United States remain faithful to the idea of international openness—even in the presence of the huge shadow cast by isolationist forces? Isolationism is just as meaningful to foreign policy as it is to economic policy.[377]

The United States inherited an inclination toward mercantilism and protectionism from the British.[378] Alexander Hamilton was a convinced protectionist, as were George Washington and Thomas Jefferson. In his famous *Report on Manufacturers* (1791), Hamilton pleaded in favor of substantial import restrictions to help develop local economic activity. Although tariffs were at first adopted to raise revenue for the government, they flourished from 1816 forward with the explicit aim of protecting infant American industries.

In 1847, Abraham Lincoln, then a member of the US Congress, declared: "Give us a protective tariff, and we will have the greatest nation on earth."[379] Another protectionist, Henry Clay (1777–1852), ran for president (unsuccessfully) five times and served as speaker of the House of Representatives and secretary of state. Clay defended protectionist policies, stating that they were also the policies of "the Edwards, of Henry the Great, of Elizabeth, of the Colberts, abroad; of our Franklin, Jefferson, Madison, Hamilton, at home."[380]

Following the Civil War, the zeal for tariffs subsided. Leading economists of the era, such as Harvard professor Frank Taussig, convincingly argued that most tariffs were counterproductive.[381] After World War I, protectionism rose again, culminating in the Smoot–Hawley Tariff Act of 1930, which was largely blamed for turning a severe recession into the Great Depression. International retaliation against America's imposition of heavy trade restrictions helped spread the Depression worldwide.

After World War II, the US government took the lead in characterizing a new world order based on open markets and free international trade. The Bretton Woods agreements led to the creation of the World Bank and the International Monetary Fund. The United States also played a crucial role in the successes achieved by the General Agreement on Tariffs and Trade and its successor, the World Trade Organization.

Two elements played a decisive role in America's defense of free trade and an open economy. First, there was a general awareness that the US's protectionist policies of the 1930s had caused tremendous damage, including leading the country into a depression and World War II. Nobody wanted to repeat those mistakes. Second, as America boasted the most developed economy in the world, it would benefit most from liberalized world economic relations and from the dollar becoming the dominant world currency. Dollar dominance gave the United States "exorbitant privilege," making it able to finance its deficits *ad infinitum*.[382] Thus, the United States naturally took the lead in keeping international sea lanes open so trade could flourish.

Although the United States has led the charge for an open international economic system since World War II, protectionist and isolationist forces persist. The Hamiltonian tradition continues. In 1998, conservative pundit Patrick Buchanan wrote:

> Behind a tariff wall built by Washington, Hamilton, Clay, Lincoln, and the Republican presidents who followed, the United States had gone from an agrarian coastal republic to become the greatest industrial power the world had ever seen—in a single century. Such was the success of the policy called protectionism that is so disparaged today.[383]

In 2010, Ian Fletcher, an economist who has worked for the US Business and Industry Council and for the Coalition for a Prosperous America, wrote the plainly titled *Free Trade Doesn't Work*.[384] According to Fletcher, "Historically, protectionism has been, in fact, the *real* American Way."[385]

Protectionist and isolationist feelings are still widespread among the American people as well. In a 2014 Pew Research Center survey, 68 percent of respondents declared that increasing trade and business ties with other countries was a good thing, while 50 percent agreed with the statement "trade destroys jobs" and 67 percent believed that "foreign companies buying domestic companies is bad."[386] The conclusion: A positive attitude toward globalization and an open economic system cannot be taken for granted among the populace of the United States. At the same time, a belief in international openness and free trade are the norm among the country's ruling elites. Temporary deviations from the decreed principles of American policymaking do occur, but at some point, correction sets in. For example, immigration policy has gone through multiple phases, careening from more openness to more restriction, and then back again. The share of the US population that was foreign born peaked at 14.8 percent in 1890, but still held at a remarkable 12.5 percent in 2009.[387]

Even if isolationism eventually gets the upper hand, the United States has the richest and most developed market economy in the world. Reduced openness toward the rest of the world will undoubtedly handicap the long-term development of the country, but it is equally true that the vastness of its internal market and the competitive nature of its internal economic system will limit the consequences of that handicap.

Furthermore, ongoing changes and advancements in ICT have ensured that the development of human capital and knowledge is unstoppable and truly internationalized. Protectionism cannot stop knowledge-based developments, and isolation from them is impossible. As Amar Bhidé, a professor at Tufts University's Fletcher School of International Affairs, has powerfully argued, the United States has all the capital markets, flexible labor market, property rights, social networks, and mass of multinational corporations it will need to absorb innovations created elsewhere in the world.[388]

Positive Polarization

In a world characterized by turbochange, opportunities to increase public welfare will grow for every country or region. As you know by now, I believe that the United States is best positioned in a world changing at turbospeed. Its readiness to accept globalization remains entrenched, and even if the influence of protectionist forces rises, their impact will be limited. Since a rise in protectionism is often an international phenomenon, given what I expect will be the limited impact of such a development in the United States, it might even reinforce the case for continued American dominance. If you lose less than your competitors do, you win.

There is a deeper level of this analysis that relates to the ability of a society to deal with the turbulence and the stress of turbochange. Typically, societies show different degrees of readiness to accept the consequences of change. It is possible to imagine a society with an impressive stock of human capital and knowledge and a strong entrepreneurial drive that nevertheless finds it difficult to deal with turbochange. To come out on top in the race, a society must excel at adaptability and change. As Gregg Easterbrook correctly noted in his book *Sonic Boom,* "those that will embrace change rather than fearing it will be the winners as decks are endlessly reshuffled."[389]

After all, as adaptability and change are hindered in a society, said society's basic capabilities in terms of human capital, knowledge, and entrepreneurship will suffer. The front-runners in knowledge development and entrepreneurial drive will always allow creative destruction inherently linked to turbochange to run its course. People with a passion for developing new ideas and entrepreneurial ventures will seek out the environment with the lowest and fewest barriers to entry. Christian Berchem, the head of Barclays Wealth, concluded that entrepreneurs "will go where the next step for their businesses takes them."[390] Being in the lead tends to induce forces that widen the lead. More than half a century ago, economic historian Albert Hirschman described this as the "polarization effect" in economic development. Development, wealth, and power tend to take place where they have already advanced most.[391]

While I believe the United States is the country best equipped to take advantage of what turbochange will offer, I want to emphasize that this is not a value judgment on it or other societies. It is the conclusion of an analytical investigation of what the world of the 21st century will be—nothing less, nothing more. I can't predict whether an American society fueled by turbospeed will be regarded as just, morally acceptable, and/or pleasant. But I can theorize about America's adaptability and positive acceptance of change.

Capacity for Change

The French sociologist and historian André Siegfried, one of the preeminent geographers of his generation, wrote in 1955 that the United States is

> an astonishing country where everything is focused on the future!... Its psychology remains characterized of a youth that we Europeans have lost. America [is] the embryo of a [distinct] civilization, which has faith in the possibility of changing the very rhythm of nature. One might also call it the great American adventure, the end of which is not in sight....[392]

Siegfried developed a keen interest in the United States and in North America in general. His remarks on the Americans' remarkable capacity for change echoed those of Alexis de Tocqueville (1805–1859), the French politician and aristocrat whose travels in the United States during the 1830s yielded the classic *Democracy in America*. Regarding his first impressions of Americans, de Tocqueville remarked that the American has no time to tie himself to anything; *he grows accustomed to naught but change* and concludes by viewing it as the natural state of man; *he feels a need for it; even more he loves it;* for instability, instead of occurring to him in the forms of disasters seem to give birth to nothing around him but wonders [italics mine].[393]

More than 50 years later, Alan Dowd, an American journalist specializing in international and security matters, agreed with de Tocqueville and Siegfried, stating:

> This is a restless nation. Its capacity for change, its desire for change, its willingness to reevaluate and reassess itself make it easy to extrapolate periodic corrections or momentary uncertainties into downward trends—declinism at its worst. Perhaps this is why its practitioners find themselves forced to revise and defer their predictions again and again.[394]

Capacity for change, willingness to reevaluate and reassess, change as the natural state of man, focus on the future—these are essential ingredients for any society to thrive in a world of turbochange. MIT scholars Erik Brynjolfsson and Andrew McAfee concluded: "Faster technological progress may ultimately bring greater wealth and longer lifespans, but it also requires faster adjustments by both people and institutions."[395]

Turbochange will lead interest groups to double down on attempts to enforce and reinforce the status quo and try to limit relative progress. As Princeton economist Angus Deaton noted, "the rich often have both the incentives and the means to block creative destruction that is required at each new round of innovation."[396] Change will come ever more quickly, and those with status will fear that it will be short lived unless they take serious action to block the change. Turbochange will intensify the fight for the relative advantage and privileged position.

Joseph Schumpeter's notion of creative destruction is a huge challenge for any society to deal in a peaceful and constructive way, as the elite few try to hold on to their privilege for dear life and emerging forces and power brokers surf the tide of creative destruction. Mancur Olson saw the outcome of this struggle between interest groups as decisive for "the rise and decline of nations" in the sense that in aging economies, special interest groups multiply and become powerful.[397] Societies that fall victim to the sclerotizing forces resulting from the infighting of interest groups will inevitably fall behind in a world changing faster and more intensely than ever before. History features a litany of tales related to this tension, which has grown exponentially since the Industrial Revolution. During the 21st century, this clash will only intensify.

Siegfried and Dowd, just as Alexis de Tocqueville long before them, are not the only ones who have suggested that the United States will thrive in the constant change of the 21st century. Lee Kuan Yew, the founding father of modern Singapore, sees a continuing prominent role for the United States because of America's "can-do approach," "entrepreneurial culture," "great urge to start new enterprises and create wealth," and the primacy that Americans accord to the "individual's interest," which makes them "more aggressively competitive."[398] Furthermore, Yew argued,

> America's strengths include an ability to range widely, imaginatively, and pragmatically; a diversity of centers of excellence that compete in inventing and embracing new ideas and new technologies, a society that attracts talent from around the world and assimilates them comfortably as Americans; and a language that is the lingua franca of those who rise to the top of their own societies around the world.[399]

According to former Secretary of the Treasury and Harvard economics professor Larry Summers, the United States has "the most flexible, entrepreneurial society the world has ever seen."[400] Jim Manzi, a serial entrepreneur and senior fellow at the Manhattan Institute, believes that the United States is best equipped for turbochange because no other country is better able to deal with "the inherent conflict between the creative destruction involved in free-market capitalism and the innate human propensity to avoid risk and change."[401] British writer and commentator Godfrey Hodgson has written extensively about "the myth of American exceptionalism," but nevertheless remarked, "I admired, and expressed my admiration at great length, for the unshakable good sense of the American majority and its capacity for righting the ship when foolish or ungenerous movements threatened its equilibrium."[402]

But there's really nothing new about America's thirst for change. On the eve of the Great Depression, presidential candidate Franklin Roosevelt explicitly referred to being ready for change, even actively seeking it out: "The country demands bold persistent experimentation. It is common sense to take a method and try it. If it fails, admit it frankly and try another. But above all, try something."[403]

Such a benign view of the US's adaptability is at odds with that of Charles Kupchan, a professor of international affairs at Georgetown University, who declared at the end of 2002 that "one of the reasons that America's moment at the top will be short-lived is that history is moving much more quickly than it used to."[404] I disagree: Because of the increasingly rapid change the world is experiencing, the United States will remain at the top.

The American Character

It is nearly tautology to state, as Daniel Gross, journalist and former senior editor of *Newsweek*, once did, that the reality-based case for optimism rests in large measure on an understanding of America's core competencies and competitive advantages: attitudes, habits, and capabilities that, even in this age of globalization, remain unique. Yes, the United States has proved in recent years that it's better than other countries at blowing systems up. But we've also learned that it's better at recovering, at recognizing and confronting new realities, at developing and executing decisive policies, at processing failure and moving on.[405]

William Wohlforth, a professor of government at Dartmouth College, remarked that the United States is gifted with a "combination of quantitative and qualitative material advantages [that] is unprecedented."[406] Stefan Halper, senior fellow at Cambridge University's Centre for International Studies, argued that "in crisis [Americans] have always found opportunity."[407] Such theses leave open many questions: What are these "core competencies and competitive advantages"? What are these "attitudes, habits, and capabilities," these "quantitative and qualitative material advantages," and this strength to find "opportunity in crisis"? Where do they come from, and what forces drive them? And can we expect them to continue to play the same roles they play now in the future?

British-born Clive Crook, a columnist and former deputy editor of *The Economist*, wrote:

The abiding source of American exceptionalism is…the American Character. This a difficult thing to quantify, hence easily dismissed, but not everything that matters can be measured. Anybody who's lived and worked in other countries can't fail to be struck by it: Americans are, above all, striving. Sloth is as antithetical to the national character as irony. Americans work incredibly hard, and they take play so seriously it's comical. They're acquisitive and competitive, but they are also friendly, as well as amazingly open to interaction with other people and to joint endeavors in business and with neighbors. With strangers, they're both welcoming and demanding…. They detest incompetence and won't settle for mediocrity. They're pragmatic—they believe in what works—yet they're reluctant to compromise. They venerate innovators and risk-takers. They see failure as a temporary setback. They expect to rely on themselves and ask the same of others. They don't think the world owes them a living…[408]

The above elements, Crook continued, go

a long way to explain America's extraordinary economic success. The same goes for the country's political institutions—themselves a result of the underlying culture. I'm not the first to notice that American culture is communitarian and individualist at the same time. There's a kind of reverence for popular sovereignty and the institutions that express it, including the Constitution and the flag, but this is combined with suspicion of government. On the one hand, "We the people." On the other, "Don't tread on me." The result, by the standards of other advanced economies, is a bound on the size and scope of the state…. All these things I admire. Admittedly, I was predisposed to admire the US, and it's true I've accentuated the positive. The same character traits produce other equally distinctive results: needlessly vituperative politics; a zeal for incarceration; legalism carried to the point of insanity—I could go on. But I'm here because I admire this country and its people, and I admire them because they're different—very different. The cultural roots, I'm certain, go deep. I'll be surprised if America doesn't stay very different for a long, long time.[409]

The bottom line: The US's economic success and pivotal role in the world order are based on an assumption that Americans have specific characteristics that differ from people from other nations. Thus, you have the concept of American "exceptionalism."[410] As James Ceaser, professor of politics at the University of Virginia, has convincingly argued, it is plainly wrong to see American exceptionalism

> as a mission...that has been shaped mainly by Puritan religious thought.... There have instead been different views influenced by different sources, including (besides religion) various philosophical doctrines, applications of scientific theories, and reasoning based on political–historical analysis.[411]

That the United States is, one way or the other, special or exceptional is a recurrent theme throughout American history. This uniqueness is often characterized by the claim that the country was "founded on ideas rather than culture or ancestry."[412]

Thomas Paine's Lineage

The first clear sign of American exceptionalism was the doctrine of manifest destiny. Harvard sociologist Daniel Bell described manifest destiny as "the civil religion of 19th century America," a blend of a total conviction that Americans were fundamentally different, compared to Europeans, and also that they were entitled to territorial rights.[413] Historian Robert Johanssen traces the origins of manifest destiny all the way back to the writings of Thomas Paine at the time of the American Revolution. Paine claimed that the settlers in North America had it in their power "to begin the world all over again.... The birthday of a new world is at hand." Johanssen characterized Paine's well-known pamphlet *Common Sense* as "the most enduring statement of America's Manifest Destiny and mission."[414]

The term itself was first used by journalist John O'Sullivan in 1845. O'Sullivan characterized the annexation of Texas as "the fulfillment of our manifest destiny to overspread the continent allotted by Providence for the free development of our yearly multiplying millions."[415] Six years previously, O'Sullivan, who was quite influential in the Democratic Party, described the United States as "the nation of many nations...destined to manifest to mankind the excellence of divine principles.... We are the nation of progress, of individual freedom, of universal enfranchisement."[416]

As early as 1782, Hector St. John de Crèvecoeur, a French immigrant to the United States, described his new compatriots as "a mixture of English, Scotch, Irish, French, Dutch, Germans, Swedes.... What, then is the American, this new man?... He is an American...leaving behind him all his ancient prejudices and manners...."[417] Alexis de Tocqueville used the word "exceptional" only once in his 700-page magnum opus *Democracy in America,* but it was a powerful instance.[418] De Tocqueville wrote,

> The situation of the Americans is therefore entirely exceptional, and it is to be believed that no [other] democratic people will ever be placed in it. Their wholly Puritan origin; their uniquely commercial habits; the very country they inhabit, which seems to turn their intelligence away from the study of the sciences, letters, and arts; the proximity of Europe, which permits them not to study these without falling back into barbarism.... Their passions, needs, education, circumstances—all in fact seem to cooperate in making the inhabitant of the United States incline toward the earth. Religion alone, from time to time, makes him raise passing, distracted glances toward Heaven.[419]

Religion is often front and center in discussions of American exceptionalism. US senator and historian Albert Beveridge was a proponent of this line of thinking; in 1900, he declared that

God "has given us the spirit of progress to overwhelm the forces of reaction throughout the earth.... And of all our races...he has marked the American people as his chosen nation to finally lead in the redemption of the world."[420] Religion's relative importance among Americans remains a striking characteristic of the country. Robert Wuthnow, a professor of social sciences at Princeton University, wrote:

> Emphasis on religion is hardly unique to the United States, but it is important in the lives of a large majority of American citizens and continues to affect public policies in ways that earlier generations of social scientists did not predict.... Presidents of both political parties routinely invoke God's blessing in addressing the nation—something that rarely happens in other Western countries.[421]

A sense of destiny, whether divinely determined or not, is integral to how the country "feels" distinct from others. In 1852 the Hungarian patriot Louis Kossuth visited the United States and concluded that

> America's destiny [is] to become the cornerstone of Liberty on earth.... Should the Republic of America ever lose this consciousness of this destiny that moment would just as surely be the beginning of America's decline as the 19th of April 1775 was the beginning of the Republic of America.[422]

President Abraham Lincoln articulated this conviction of destiny in his annual message to Congress on December 1, 1862, as the Civil War raged on. In it, he described the United States as "the last best hope of man on earth."[423] John Winthrop, one of the earliest English settlers in the New World, claimed that the British colony would be "the city on the hill" and that "the eyes of all the people are upon us."[424]

Early 20th century German economist Werner Sombart investigated another aspect of American exceptionalism—the fact that socialism and communism never really got off the ground in the United States. Sombart concluded that the lack of interest in these systems existed in large part because "I believe that emotionally the American worker has a share in capitalism: I believe that he loves it."[425] According to Sombart, Americans believe that capitalism is the basis of the Constitution—and that thus, no other system is up for discussion.

The US's immunity to socialism and communism also drew the attention of Soviet dictator Josef Stalin. In 1929, American communist leader Jay Lovestone informed Stalin that the American proletariat was not really interested in Marxism and the anti-capitalist revolution. Stalin responded with a mixture of anger and incomprehension to Lovestone's message, instructing him to take action in order to end this "heresy of American exceptionalism."[426] According to Daniel Rodgers, a professor of history at Princeton University, "exceptionalism" was the banner under which Stalin cast all of America's abnormalities.[427]

The Outlier

Gunnar Myrdal, the Swedish economist, sociologist, and politician who won the Nobel Prize in Economics in 1974, brought a new element to the discussion on American exceptionalism. When investigating race relations in mid-20th century America, Myrdal concluded that political and social interaction in the United States was largely determined by what he labeled as the American creed.[428] The American melting pot—whites and blacks, rich and poor, native born and new immigrants—functioned quite well, Myrdal argued, because of this American creed: the ideals of liberty, equality, justice, hard work, and fair treatment of all people.[429] The American creed, which is based on 18th-century Enlightenment philosophy, is clearly present in the Declaration of Independence, specifically its second paragraph: "We hold these truths to be self-evident, that all men are created equal, that they are endowed by their Creator with certain unalienable Rights, that among these are Life, Liberty and the pursuit of Happiness."

Seymour Martin Lipset (1922–2006), one of America's most prominent political sociologists, continued Myrdal's concept of the American creed in his seminal book *American Exceptionalism: A Double-Edged Sword*. Lipset redefined it as consisting of five elements:

> liberty, egalitarianism, individualism, populism, and laissez-faire.... These values reflect the absence of feudal structures, monarchies and aristocracies.... The emphasis in the American value system, in the American Creed, has been on the individual. Citizens have been expected to demand and protect their rights on a personal basis.... Americans remain much more individualistic, meritocratic-oriented, and anti-statist than people elsewhere. Hence, the values which form the context for public policy are quite different from those in other developed countries....[430]

Being exceptional, Lipset argued, "does not mean better." It makes the United States "an outlier...the most religious, optimistic, patriotic, rights-oriented, and individualistic [nation]."[431] Lipset defined exceptionalism as

> something of a double-edged sword: it fosters a high sense of personal responsibility, independent initiative, and voluntarism even as it encourages self-serving behavior, atomism, and a disregard for communal good. More specifically, its emphasis on individualism threatens traditional forms of community morality, and thus

has historically promoted a particularly virulent strain of greedy behavior. At the same time, it represents a tremendous asset, encouraging the self-reflection necessary for responsible judgment, for fostering the strength of voluntary communal and civic bonds, for principled opposition to wars, and for patriotism.[432]

Author Peter Conrad also explicitly referred to the double edge:

Americans can be at once innocent and ruthless, naïve and cruel. Without such a combination of opposite qualities, they could never have survived, let alone prevailed: the country they thought of as a paradise regained was a wilderness that had to be subjugated by axes and guns, with faith backed up by force.[433]

Yale Law School's Peter Schuck and James Wilson, a professor of government at Harvard University, concluded their 2008 book *Understanding America: The Anatomy of an Exceptional Nation* with a summary of what constitutes American exceptionalism:

The individualism of the people, the productivity and flexibility of the economy, and the power of its popular culture feed mass consumerism, but this consumerism is tempered by deep patriotism and a strong commitment to civil liberties, even in times of war. The constitutionally constrained reach of the government limits the amount of money spent on welfare, but this limited government helps to encourage a strong interest in religion and an unparalleled commitment to private philanthropy and voluntary organizations providing a vast array of social services to the poor. Americans distrust many of their governmental institutions but venerate their Constitution and the personal freedoms that it protects, freedoms that in turn create and shape these public institutions.... This country is not an odd mixture of Paris Hilton, Pat Robertson, and rob-

ber barons.... America's main problems today...are the
large and unfortunate costs of freedom, and freedom is
America's watchword.[434]

To me, this idea of an American character seems more appropriate and useful than American exceptionalism. Every country or
region—and every man or woman—is exceptional in some way.
US President Barack Obama expressed a similar view, stating: "I
believe in American exceptionalism, just as I suspect that the Brits
believe in British exceptionalism and the Greeks believe in Greek
exceptionalism."[435] My preference for the term "American character"
does not mean that elements from the discussion on American
exceptionalism are not useful—quite the opposite is true. Many
things human are unique, and thus exceptional.

"Self-Interest Well Understood"

The analyses of de Tocqueville, Sombart, Myrdal, Siegfried, Lipset,
and Schuck and Wilson enumerated many specific characteristics
unique to America and Americans, features that make the country
and its citizens different from others. The most frequently cited
characteristics include a strong preference for, if not outright de-
votion to, equality, liberty, justice, egalitarianism, populism, laissez-faire, hard work, patriotism, individualism, constitutionalism,
spirit for citizenship, and religiosity.[436]

So there are four building blocks essential to my argument
for the relevance of the American character to coping with turbochange. I define them as *the constitutional and geographic starting
point* the nation benefited from, which led to a *widespread acceptance of the laissez-faire system or the free-market economy, the frontier dimension* deeply ingrained in country's very essence, and its
people and *the immigration impulse* so crucial to keep the American system's wheels turning. These forces build upon each other to
create an environment in which change is not only welcomed but

in fact feverishly sought. America's heritage and history have created institutional, political, social, and economic conditions that we need to thrive in the age of turbochange.

The American Constitution, in combination with the Bill of Rights and the Declaration of Independence, turned all ideas about citizens' rights up until that point in history on their head. In the past, and pretty much everywhere else in the world, rights and liberties were entirely dependent on the grace and consent of the ruler or government. They could be awarded, but also changed or withdrawn, by that same ruler or government without the citizenry having any say in that process.

The Constitution explicitly states that the American people inherently possess natural rights that must be respected by the authorities and hence constrains those authorities' actions and degrees of freedom. Violation of these rights gives the people the right to supplant a government "destructive of these ends,"[437] which historian Arthur Schlesinger has singled out as the most important American contribution to civilization. This (literally) revolutionary approach, inspired by the intellectual heritage of the Age of Enlightenment and democratizing developments in Great Britain, was a result of the Founding Fathers' resolve to do things differently.[438]

The federal/state structure of the United States diffuses power among many branches of government. From its very start, the American system had decentralization written all over it. Also the American legal system has always been oriented toward protection of individual rights, often at the expense of government claims.[439] This political and legal system focused on inalienable individual rights has long stimulated innovation and experimentation. As author Peter Conrad wrote, "Americans continue to do a disproportionate amount of the world's scientific and technological thinking: *innovation is their national mission* [italics mine]."[440] An assurance of respect for personal rights and an accompanying rule of law promote initiative, entrepreneurship, and risk taking throughout American society.

Of course, many other countries followed America's lead and included individual rights in their constitutions, but in the late 18th century, this very new approach found itself in economically fertile territory—most importantly, thanks to the benevolent geographical characteristics of North America's core. The natural transport system of the Greater Mississippi Basin played a crucial role:

> [It] allowed early settlers to quickly obtain their own small tracts of land. It was an attractive option that helped fuel the early migration waves into the United States and then into the continent's interior. Growing ranks of landowners exported their agricultural output either back…to the East Coast or down the Ohio and Mississippi rivers and on to Europe…. Small towns formed as wealth collected in the new territories, and in time the wealth accumulated to the point that portions of the United States had the capital necessary to industrialize…. The attraction of owning one's own destiny made [the United States] the destination of choice for most European migrants….[441]

An overwhelming constitutional emphasis on individual rights, easy accessibility to fertile territory, and a laissez-faire system characterized by a business culture dominated by individual entrepreneurs and small companies were highly attractive to the new settlers and their offspring. The American character began to take shape, and with it came a feeling that life would continuously get better with the passage of time, via hard work and dedication. Analysts from the strategic consulting firm Stratfor wrote that the country's specific constitutional and geographic configuration nudged the United States toward a laissez-faire that rewards efficiency and a political culture that encourages entrepreneurship. It is also clear how geography has created distributed economic centers, transportation corridors and a massive internal market and provided easy access to both of the world's great trading basins. Byproducts of this are a culture that responds well to change and an economy characterized by stable, long-term growth without being dependent on external support.[442]

Alexis de Tocqueville devoted a chapter of *Democracy in America* to America's acceptance of laissez-faire or free-market economics. The very title of the chapter indicated how curious de Tocqueville found it: "How the Americans Combat Individualism by the Doctrine of Self-Interest Well Understood."[443] De Tocqueville argued about the doctrine of self-interest well understood that

> among Americans of our day it has been universally accepted...one finds it at the foundation of all actions; it pierces into all discussions. It is encountered not less in the mouth of the poor man than in that of the rich.... Americans are pleased to explain almost all the actions of their life with the aid of self-interest well understood.... Self-interest well understood is a doctrine not very lofty but clear and sure.... Each American knows how to sacrifice a part of his particular interests to save the rest.[444]

That Frontier Thing

The Constitution specified the absolute preeminence of individual rights for the first time in human history; settlers seized this idea and saw it as a font of limitless opportunity to better their lives and the lives of their children. Improved living conditions and working conditions that promoted well-being were actively sought after.

This configuration so conducive to change became part and parcel of the American character. The buildup of the American DNA, however, did not stop there.

"Farewell, the new frontier," conservative commentator Charles Krauthammer wrote on the day the space shuttle Discovery flew its final flight in April 2012; Krauthammer also wondered whether there could be "a better symbol of willed American decline?"[445] Two years earlier, the same commentator fulminated against "Closing the New Frontier" that John F. Kennedy had opened.[446] When accepting the Democratic Party's nomination for the presidency in 1960, Kennedy titled his speech "The New Frontier," arguing that

> we stand today at the edge of a New Frontier—the frontier of the 1960s, the frontier of unknown opportunities and perils, the frontier of unfilled hopes and unfilled threats. Beyond that frontier are uncharted areas of science and space, unsolved problems of peace and war, unconquered problems of ignorance and prejudice, unanswered questions of poverty and surplus....[447]

President Obama had stated intentions of continuing space exploration; shutting down the Discovery program was in sharp contrast to these plans, so conservatives like Krauthammer protested. The heated discussion surrounding Discovery's end clearly showed how important the image of a frontier, and of constantly charging against that frontier, had become to the United States of America. Jack Forbes, a historian at the University of Nevada, wrote, "Looming large upon the American historical horizon has always been the subject of frontiers."[448]

Over time, the frontier became a prominent symbol of what American culture and society stood for—especially a relentless search for what Kennedy called "unknown opportunities." Charging against the frontier inevitably demanded constant change to the economic structure and the organization of society. The fron-

tier helped shape the American character in two great waves—
geographic and then scientific.

American historian Frederick Jackson Turner (1861–1932) developed the "frontier thesis," which essentially claimed that what
distinguished America and Americans from others was the country's constant westward progression toward the frontier.[449] Turner
first delivered his thesis at a meeting of historians in Chicago in
1893. It is to the frontier experience, Turner wrote, that

> the American intellect owes its striking characteristics.
> That coarseness and strength combined with acute-
> ness and inquisitiveness; that practical, inventive turn
> of mind, quick to find expedients: that masterful grasp
> of material things, lacking in the artistic but powerful
> to effect great ends; that restless, nervous energy, that
> dominant individualism, working for good and for evil,
> and withal that buoyancy and exuberance which comes
> with freedom—these are the traits of the frontier, or
> traits called our elsewhere because of the existence of
> the frontier.[450]

According to Turner, the frontier experience necessitated "pe-
rennial rebirth" of American life and social development, "[fur-
nishing] the forces dominating American character."[451] Turner an-
ticipated that once the natural frontier reached its geographical
limit, the concept would continue to develop in other directions:

> Since the days when the fleet of Columbus sailed into
> the waters of the New World, America has been another
> name for opportunity, and the people of the United
> States have taken their tone from the incessant expan-
> sion which has not only been open but has even been
> forced upon them. He would be a rash prophet who
> should assert that the expansive character of American
> life has now entirely ceased.... The American energy
> will continually demand a wider shift for its exercise.[452]

As Turner wrote these words, the second stage of the frontier experience was already developing, and scientific progress was the heart and soul of it. In the wake of the Industrial Revolution, scientific progress went into high gear in the United States, not only in the development of basic scientific knowledge but also in its practical applications.[453]

The search for new scientific knowledge entered the frontier lexicon by way of director of the Office of Scientific Research and Development Vannevar Bush's report to then–US president Franklin Roosevelt. Roosevelt sought Bush's recommendations on scientific progress and the government policies necessary to support it. According to Roosevelt, "new frontiers of the mind are before us, and if they are pioneered with the same vision, boldness, and drive with which we have waged this war, we can create a fuller and more fruitful employment and a fuller and more fruitful life."[454] Bush's report to was titled "Science—The Endless Frontier."[455] In his Letter of Transmittal, Bush concluded:

> The pioneer spirit is still vigorous within this Nation. Science offers a largely unexplored hinterland for the pioneer who has the tools for this task. The rewards of such exploration both for the Nation and the individual are great. Scientific progress is one essential key to our security as a nation, to our better health, to more jobs, to a higher standard of living, and to our cultural progress.[456]

The idea of science as an endless frontier has proven to be true. An exponentially growing stock of human capital, feverish entrepreneurial drive, and increased globalization are leading to turbo-change, which in turn pushes out the frontier in all directions. In many countries and regions, the frontier concept is rather unfamiliar territory. In these areas, progress has largely only come about by catching up (at least to some degree) in terms of technological and applied scientific knowledge and economic advancement. The United States has been in front—*on the frontier*—for most of the 20th century and certainly now, at the start of the 21st century. Transitioning from challenging the physical, geographical frontier ("going West") to the endless scientific frontier has come quite naturally to the United States and its people.

"Makers, Not Takers"

A revolutionary constitution focused on individual rights, a benign geographical environment, and its frontier experience enabled the United States to quickly rise to international power. Keeping the machine going was the country's openness to new immigrants, the fourth pillar of the American character. What historian Arthur Schlesinger concluded in 1959 remains very much true in the 21st century: "The constant infusion of new blood has enriched our cultural life, speeded our material progress, and produced some of our ablest statesmen.... The American achievement stands alone in its scale, thoroughness, and rapidity of the process."[457] In 1915, President Woodrow Wilson defined the constant flow of immigrants into the country as a unique experience of "constant and repeated rebirth.... This country is constantly drawing strength out of new sources."[458]

The United States began as a nation of immigrants. Almost by definition, immigration *equals* change. It brings in new people, most of them searching to make their lives better and committed to doing whatever it takes to achieve that. Yale Law School's Peter Schuck correctly noted that

> of all the features of American society that distinguish the United States from other liberal democracies, immigration is perhaps the most far-reaching. It drives the demography, infuses religiosity, populates cities, expands the economy, affects schools and other public services, influences foreign policies and constructs the

future of our constitutional community by constantly altering the composition of "We, the People."[459]

When the first settlers arrived in North America, the indigenous population was estimated at about 500,000. By 1790, the continent's population had grown to 4 million. A century later, it stood at 63 million. Of course, some of the increase in population came from Africans whose immigration was forced through bondage, but most of the immigrants came from Europe. Immigration was essentially unrestricted during the country's first century of existence, but migration laws became more restrictive after World War I. During the 1960s, both legal and illegal immigration from Latin America, Caribbean nations, and Asia greatly increased the diversity of America's demographics.

Over time, public discussion on immigration went through a variety of phases, positive attitudes alternating more frequently with pessimistic and negative opinions.[460] Since the terrorist attacks of 9/11, public animosity toward immigrants has grown, and policies have become more restrictive.[461] Several studies have even questioned whether immigrants really contribute to America's economy and society in general, and their findings are reflective of anti-immigration feelings and attitudes.[462]

Evidence remains strong that "immigrants are makers, not takers."[463] Canadian diplomat Colin Robertson wrote, "Hispanics today bring a tremendous amount of capacity, just as the Irish of the 1830s, '40s, and '50s did, and the Italians in the 1920s and 1930s, all of whom have made a huge contribution to America's economy."[464] Immigrants also tend to be young, which helps the United States edge out other advanced countries whose populations are aging.

Entrepreneurs like Facebook's Mark Zuckerberg lobby intensively to obtain visas for skilled workers. In fact, 40 percent or more of the high-tech companies located in New Jersey, Massachusetts, and California were founded by immigrants; the average for the United States as a whole is close to 25 percent.[465] These companies are not only important for the technological push and pull they bring about but also for the jobs they create. As *The Economist* noted:

> High-tech firms such as Google (whose co-founder Sergey Brin moved to America from Russia as a child) haven't just created jobs for their own workers. They have also inspired the creation of entirely new categories of job. A few years ago no one earned a living as a mobile-app developer. Now they are everywhere. [466]

Clearly, immigrant entrepreneurs and workers play a central part in the change that turbochange brings about.[467]

Despite recent animosity regarding immigration issues, including public resistance against immigration and heated political debate, the fact remains that the United States still has one of the most open immigration policies in the world. In 2008, Peter Schuck concluded:

> The United States continues to be the world's strongest magnet for the talented, the ambitious, the dispossessed, and the desperate. It remains a country with immense assimilative capacity, which however strained never seems fully exhausted. Not only are immigrants essential to America's soft and hard power in the world; perhaps more important, most Americans appreciate this fact, and recurrent political efforts to limit immigration almost invariably fail.... [Legal and undocumented] migration...sustain a mythos of rebirth and revitalization in America that never ceases to astonish.[468]

Rebirth and revitalization—exactly the characteristics a nation needs to thrive in turbochange. The US's openness to immigration will contribute in important ways to its future success.

Nasty Politics

The materially—and mentally—important concept of a frontier with "unknown opportunities" has long powered the engine of American industriousness and economic progress. A similar effect results from the constant push and pull caused by a continuous influx of immigrants. These characteristics of the American character make the country best equipped to deal with turbochange.

So all is going well for the United States—or is it? Well, I do have some reservations about this overall optimistic scenario. America's fundamentally sound starting position may experience pressure from three issues: political deadlock, debt, and inequality.

Historian and foreign policy specialist Robert Kagan remarked:

> One thing does seem clear from the historical evidence: the American system, for all its stultifying qualities, has [also] shown a greater capacity to adapt and recover from difficulties than that of many other nations, including its geopolitical competitors. This undoubtedly has something to do with the relative freedom of the society, which rewards innovators, often outside the existing power structure, for producing new ways of doing things, and relatively open political system, which allows movements to gain steam and influence the behavior of the political establishment. The American system is slow and clunky in part because the Founders designed it that way, with a federal system, checks and balances, and a written Constitution and Bill of Rights. But the system also possesses a remarkable ability to undertake changes just when the steam kettle looks about to blow its lid.[469]

Despite Kagan's optimism, it's hard to deny that deadlock and dysfunction currently pervade American politics.[470] When, as *Washington Post* columnist E.J. Dionne argued, "journeys to the fiscal brink [have become] as commonplace as summertime visits to the beach or the ballpark," it's reasonable to see the situation as a "permanent crisis"[471] or, in the words of Georgetown University history professor Michael Kazin, a "deadlocked mess."[472] During the 2012 presidential election, *Time* magazine claimed that "taming a dysfunctional political system will be the next President's first priority."[473] Some commentators have concluded that "our political system is flawed and no longer benefits Americans,"[474] that America has a huge problem with "political legitimacy,"[475] and/or that "America's political consensus can no longer address the country's most basic problems."[476]

The American political system's structural problems are manifold. The extreme fringe (for example, the Tea Party on the right and the Occupy movement on the left) are polarizing and blocking meaningful compromises. The system of political financing is growing ever shadier. Special interest groups can have a paralyzing effect on legislation. There is little in the way of courageous leadership focused on the long term. The hypercompetitive, oversensationalized, oversimplified, and overconsumed landscape of politics leads observers only to hear what they want to hear, and little in terms of dissent.

Although systemic dysfunction seems to characterize the American political scene, I agree with Kagan, who provides some historic perspective:

> There have been many times over the past two centuries when the political system was dysfunctional, hopelessly gridlocked, and seemingly unable to find solutions to crushing national problems—from slavery and then Reconstruction, to the dislocations of industrialization at the end of the nineteenth century and the crisis of social welfare during the Great Depression, to the confusions and paranoia of the early Cold War years. Anyone who honestly recalls the 1970s, with Watergate, Vietnam, stagflation, and the energy crisis, cannot really believe the present difficulties are unrivalled.[477]

Joseph Nye of the John F. Kennedy School of Government at Harvard University adds,

> Nasty politics is nothing new—as John Adams, Alexander Hamilton, and Thomas Jefferson could attest. Part of the problem with assessing the current atmosphere is that trust in government became abnormally high among the generation that survived the Depression and won World War II.... The country's past cultural battles, over immigration, slavery, evolution, temperance, McCarthyism, and Civil Rights, were arguably more serious than any of today's.[478]

James DeLong of the Competitive Enterprise Institute is of like mind.

> The United States has always been an exceptional society, and it may be a pioneer in reviving [political] legitimacy, just as it was a pioneer in its original constitutional arrangements.... We have the intellectual tools to understand and analyze the reality that we have a legitimacy crisis.[479]

Two other major problems facing the United States in the early phases of the 21st century are the debt and the inequality issues. Tackling these two problems in a significant way would cure to a considerable degree the "permanent crisis" of the "dysfunctional political system" that many today see as something of an existential threat to the American character.

Bankrupt, but Less So than Others

"If the US does not put its house in order, the reckoning will be sure and the devastation will be severe.... After all the talk about debts and deficits, it is long time past for America's leaders to put up or shut up. The era of debt denial is over..." Such was the conclusion of a 2010 report by the National Commission on Fiscal Responsibility and Reform.[480] Boston University economics professor Laurence Kotlikoff, a leading specialist on long-term sustainability of public finances, took this sentiment a step further: "US is bankrupt and we don't even know it.... The US is in worse fiscal shape than Greece."[481] Herb Stein, chairman of US President Richard Nixon's Council of Economic Advisers, once famously noted that "something that can't go on, will stop." An increasing number of analysts and commentators see the future of American debt, and certainly public debt, as Stein's dictum come true.[482]

But do the hard data on American debt support this? Since the start of the 21st century, American gross public debt more than doubled in relation to the size of the economy. According to data from the OECD, it escalated from 48.1 percent of GDP in 2000 to 109.2 percent of GDP at the end of 2013. In nominal dollars, American public debt almost tripled, from $5.7 trillion to $16.7 trillion. The wars in Afghanistan and Iraq, the buildup of a homeland security department following the events of 9/11, the financial and banking crisis, and the ensuing deep recession are most often blamed for the run-up of debt, but this thesis isn't backed up by the data.[483] The combined cost of the wars in Iraq and Afghanistan, for example, accounted for no more than 10 percent to 15 percent of the annual deficit.

Things get worse if you survey the debt figure for the American economy as a whole. At the end of 2013, total debt stood at 362 percent of GDP, with government at 105 percent, the financial sector at 98 percent, nonfinancial companies at 81 percent, and households at 79 percent.[484] Of the total American debt, 73 percent is held domestically and 27 percent is held by foreigners.

These data are impressive, but they in no way portray the United States as a dangerous outlier. On the contrary: Debtwise, the United States is pretty average. At the end of 2013, overall debt in all developed countries stood at 385 percent of GDP—

22 percentage points of GDP higher than the number for the United States alone. At the top is Ireland (1,026), followed by the Netherlands (636), Japan (562), Portugal (507), the UK (495), Sweden (422), Belgium (408), Spain (394), and Canada (374).

In developed countries, overall debt averages at 63 percent held domestically and 37 percent held by foreigners; many allege that the percentage of US debt that is held by foreigners is a serious problem, but if that's true, other countries have a much bigger problem. If you consider only public debt, the United States' level of 105 percent of GDP is very close to the average among developed nations, which is 108 percent. Countries with higher public debt ratios include Japan (243), Greece (175), Portugal (129), and Ireland (124).

While American debt rates are very high by historical peacetime standards, this clearly indicates that the United States is certainly not the worst off among developed countries.[485] But the United States shouldn't take comfort in these comparative debt data. There's no scientific way to determine the exact amount of maximum debt burden a country can support, but it's obvious that the level of government debt has potential to destabilize the economy, currency, capital markets, and international relations.[486] Moreover, continuous budget deficits and high debt levels make it increasingly difficult for the American government to address critical areas like education and infrastructure, such as roads, bridges, ports, rail, and networks that could use a substantial injection of new investment.[487]

If the American public debt situation requires action right now, what the future holds only increases the need for urgency. To understand this perspective, it's important to realize what factors drive American debt dynamics. Social Security, Medicare, Medicaid, and other health care are spending already main drivers of total government expenditures, but as the Baby Boomers age, this stress will only increase. For example, economists at the

Bank for International Settlements produced remarkable projections of how, if policies do not change, public health care and pension spending will change between 2013 and 2040. For the United States, the projected overall increase in spending amounts to 9 percent of GDP—with health care spending accounting for close to 80 percent of the increase. Among developed countries, only South Korea's expected health care and pension outlays will increase more.[488] If policies do not change drastically, Kotlikoff and other pessimistic economists will be proven right. For Americans and their political leaders, a moment of truth on fiscal matters is arriving soon.

Inequality Time

So what about rising inequality? At the end of 2013, US President Barack Obama defined inequality as "the defining challenge of our time...a fundamental threat to the American dream."[489] According to Nobel Prize–winning economist Joe Stiglitz of Columbia University, Americans are paying a high price for increasing inequality:

> An economic system that is less stable and less efficient, with less growth, and a democracy that has been put into peril. But even more is at stake: as our economic system is seen to fail for most citizens, and as our political system seems to be captured by moneyed interests, confidence in our democracy and in our market economy will erode along with our global influence.[490]

Serial entrepreneur Jim Manzi regards "the growing bifurcation of America" as very worrisome. He adds, "Our country is [increasingly] segregated into high-income groups with a tendency to bourgeois norms, and low-income groups experiencing profound social breakdown."[491] Harvard political scientist and sociologist Robert Putnam sees a loss of equality of opportunity as fundamentally un-American: "The fundamental bargain, the core of America, has always been that we can live with big gaps between rich and poor as long as there is also equality of opportunity. If that is no longer true, the core bargain is violated."[492]

Substantial increases in inequality in the United States can be seen in many ways; perhaps the most impressive is the increasing discrepancy between average income and median income. Average income is total income divided by the total number of people, and real GDP per capita is most often used to capture this average income. Median income is the income of the person exactly in the middle of the income distribution, meaning that there are exactly as many people earning more than that person as there are people earning less. If average income increases more than median income, the income distribution is less equal. The data speak for themselves. Taking 1975 as the base year, real median income increased only by 20 percent by 2010; in the same period, average income increased by more than 80 percent.[493]

Several other indicators point in the same direction.[494] The share of income going to the top 1 percent of Americans stood at around 11 percent in the years after World War II. It declined to 8 percent by the late 1970s and then rose to 18 percent by 2012. Real income growth over the period 1947–2012 was around 100 percent for the four lowest percentiles and 200 percent for the top 20 percent (the two highest percentiles), with close to 300 percent going to the top 1 percent. The change in real wages from 1973 to 2012 was basically zero for the 10th to the 50th percentile of the wage distribution, and the increase in real wages over the same period ranged from 6 percent in the 60th percentile to 31 percent in the 90th percentile. In terms of wealth distribution, the very rich did quite well despite the financial crisis. According to *Forbes*, the combined net worth of its billionaire list has more than quintupled in real terms since the start of the 21st century.

Where does this rise in inequality come from? The most frequently cited villains include politicians changing the tax system in favor of the rich, globalization and foreign competition, and Wall Street and the bank(st)ers—but none of these is the real cause. The main driver behind rising inequality is skill-biased technological change. Modern technology creates specific winners in terms of income distribution, particularly among those with specific quantities of human capital; superstars in media, sports, and entertainment; top CEOs; and the upper echelons of lawyers.[495] Modern technology leads to more advantages for these specific groups via the digitization of ever more information, goods, and services; the enormous improvement in telecommunications; and the increased importance of networks.[496]

Yet the issue of increasing inequality is nuanced.[497] First of all, the trend toward larger inequality is noticeable not only in the United States but also in most other advanced countries. Even in societies that have been known to have relatively equal income and wealth distributions (e.g., Scandinavian countries), inequality has risen substantially during the last two decades. These societies remain more equal than the American one, but the increase in inequality is remarkably similar.[498] Second, standard statistics on income do not take into account price decreases and quality improvements, two factors that benefit those at the lower end of the income distribution.[499] Third, the idea that the rich stay rich and get even richer while the poor stay poor and get even poorer isn't really supported by the data. For example, in an analysis on upward and downward mobility in the American income distribution, Gerald Auten, Geoffrey Gee, and Nicholas Turner of the Office of Tax Analysis of the US Treasury Department concluded that over a period of 20 years (1987–2007) "most low-income children were in higher relative positions than their parents."[500] Moreover,

> the long term changing of the guard at the top of the distribution is illustrated by the fact that the pre-boomer "Greatest Generation" and "Silent Generation" together

accounted for 79 percent of the top 1 percent in 1987, but their share had fallen to 22 percent by 2010. Their places were taken by the Baby Boom generations whose combined shares rose from 21 to 59 percent over this period. Analysis of short-term persistence in the top 1 percent found that 37 to 47 percent dropped out after one year. From 41 to 49 percent were again in the top 1 percent five years later, and 23 to 31 percent had remained there for six consecutive years.[501]

Most importantly, the standard way of looking at income and income distributions misses very important points in terms of *real* distribution of income. Gary Burtless of the liberal think-tank Brookings Institution, writing about data released by the Congressional Budget Office, came to a surprising conclusion:

> What the CBO statistics do *not* show, however, is that middle- and low-income families have failed to share in the nation's long-term prosperity. Over the past one-, two- and three-decade periods, both middle income class and poor households have experienced noticeable gains in living standards.[502]

The main reason for this unexpected conclusion: The most commonly used indicators of income focus solely on before-tax cash income. Hence, they fail to account for changes in the tax burden and the effects of transfers. Burtless felt this confirmed the trend toward greater inequality but warned that

> what many observers miss, however, is the success of the nation's tax and transfer systems in protecting low- and middle-income Americans.... As a result of these programs, the spendable incomes of poor and middle class families have been better insulated against the recession-driven losses than the incomes of Americans in the top 1 percent.[503]

The American Way

If your focus is on the general well-being of its people, America's political system is not functioning well. As a consequence of this political dysfunction, the debt problem has become a permanent crisis with a recurrent debt ceiling circus as the cherry on top. Although the equality issue is largely caused by skill-biased technological developments, more courageous political decision making could make a significant difference. The lack of constructive political action has also hurt US immigration policy—which in turn hurts the economy.

As scholars Joseph Nye and Robert Kagan have noted, the American political process is something of a mess. The delicate balance of power among the different entities of the American state inevitably becomes outrageously slow, inefficient, and even counterproductive from time to time. Because of the transparency and democratic nature of the government's processes, all involved are constantly forced into open discussion and soul-searching. There's no way to hide or deny that there is a problem, and it can take time to come up with solutions and progress. But the pressure and drive in that direction are relentless. Even when the system seems utterly broken, under the surface, the needed change, or at least parts of it, is slowly taking shape.

Winston Churchill has been credited with the remark, "You can always count on the Americans to do the right thing—after they have tried everything else." It usually takes a very long time for political decision making to effectively tackle the problems of American society, with considerable fallout: damage; unrest; and wasted time, energy, and money. But, history teaches us, the system eventually corrects, thanks to what I call the American character: the Constitution's system of private rights and rule of law, an unswerving belief in laissez-faire governance and a free-market economy, the frontier mentality, and the constant influx of new immigrants. As long as these elements remain intact—and my conclusion is that they will—I have no doubt that the United States will prevail. The American system constantly invites change. Its history is littered with evidence of its resilience. But isn't it a possibility that other nations can "catch up" and thrive in turbochange?

Chapter 4

The Runner(s)-Up

THE 20TH CENTURY BELONGED TO THE UNITED STATES. During that time, it climbed to world dominance. Its massive, strong economy supported the buildup of military power beyond any in the history of mankind, considerably weakening the classic argument that empires always overreach in their ambitions and perceived duties.[504] Its democratic system, popular culture, and open society attracted immigrants, making it dominant in terms of soft power as well. The underlying driving force behind this evolution was and is the American character, a blend of historical, institutional, economic, sociologic, and cultural elements. It is this American character that makes it well equipped to thrive in a demanding world of turbochange.

Yet tales of America's coming decline abound. Today, the prevailing wisdom is that America's stay at the top of the heap has come to an end, or at least that the end is nigh. Most of these arguments conclude that China will inevitably be the superpower, but I prefer to first examine the challenger that once seemed best poised to overtake the United States: the European Union.

Union Adrift

During the first years of the 21st century, several scholars, analysts, and politicians claimed that the EU was well placed to dominate in world affairs.[505] The initial success of the monetary union and its euro fed speculations that Europe would become more and more integrated and that integration would fuel its rise to power.[506] The initial success of the euro experiment, it was believed, powerfully countered the claim that "by the turn of the millennium, at the latest, it should have been clear that Europe was no longer on the road to superpower status, but that it faced an existential crisis."[507] An increasingly unified EU would become the largest economy in the world, drawing on massive reserves of human capital, a well-designed social welfare state, great educational systems, well-developed capital markets, and an impressive cultural heritage. And decisive political clout in world affairs would follow that economic power.

Of course, the euro crisis—an accident waiting to happen[508]— dealt a severe blow to the prospect of a truly unified Europe. And why was it an accident waiting to happen? Some of the basic rules of creating an efficient and durable monetary union were violated from the very beginning. In hindsight, it's quite surprising that it took 10 years for these failures to produce a major crisis.[509] When the euro region faltered in 2010, Greece quickly became the epicenter of the crisis, and policymakers were not ready for the challenge. As a matter of fact, it took the most important policymakers as long as two years to accept the fact that fundamental reform was necessary. The chaotic and divisive crisis management that ensued crushed dreams of further European unification.

The details of the euro crisis can be found in another book (specifically, my 2011 book *The End of the Euro*), but I mention it for the purposes of this book because it highlighted the fundamental flaws of a truly unified Europe. A monetary union can only be efficient and durable if all its participants follow the rules.

This is possible only if sufficient authority is transferred from the level of the nation-state to the level relevant for the working of the monetary union—in this case, the European level. That transfer of authority was not possible at the beginning of the European monetary union, in 1999, because its largest member states (namely, Germany, France, and Italy) were unwilling to accept an irrevocable loss of national authority.

The unspoken expectation: Once the monetary union was operational, it would quickly become obvious that the transfer of authority was inevitable. Political action would automatically transpire and bring about the desired results. The late Belgian prime minister Jean-Luc Dehaene often argued that further European integration needed crisis situations to be able to proceed; his argument was commonly accepted by European policymakers at the time.

When the euro crisis struck, of course, this line of reasoning turned out to be something close to wishful thinking. Once the crisis came close to destroying the monetary union—as it did at the end of 2011 and in the early months of 2012—at last, steps were taken to avoid a prolonged period of chaos and decline.[510] Yet as soon as the darkest hours of the crisis passed, the euro zone quickly went back to business as usual—squelching hope of further progress toward institutional completion of the monetary union.

The euro crisis revealed the fundamental obstacle in the path of a more unified Europe: Most nation-states are unwilling to relinquish their national authority in a substantive and definitive way. Hence, a truly unified European Union that can compete with the United States is quite unlikely. If anything, the euro crisis shed light on just how insurmountable the differences between groups of member states were in terms of their vision for economic, financial, and social policies. Political parties with a euro-skeptical perspective, and those that outright reject the idea of European unification, have gained considerable traction in almost all member states. As a result, the idea of the EU as truly challenging the United States is less likely than it has been at any point since World War II.

Moreover, no matter what constructive steps are taken toward further European integration in the years ahead, it remains doubtful that a unified Europe would be well equipped to thrive in turbochange. Alberto Alesina and Francesco Giavazzi, professors of economics at Harvard University and Bocconi University in Milan, respectively, correctly diagnosed the major shortcoming of the European social and economic model as one that overemphasizes protection. In their view, European policymakers promise protection all the time:

> Protection from Chinese imports, protection from the cultural diversity that comes with immigration, protection from the superior technology of some American firms, protection of university jobs, protection of small shopkeepers, of wealthy notary publics, of the unemployed, of the poor, of the old.... The word "protection" can have a positive connotation: protection of the weaker, protection from aggression, protection from adversity. But the kind of protection to which we are referring is of a different nature. It is the protection of insiders, of those who are connected, at the expense of those who would benefit from more competition. It is the protection of the few against the interests of the many.[511]

Efforts to restructure this model and make it more flexible and more receptive to change have been at best partially successful; the German reforms of the early 2000s were among the most successful. In an environment of turbochange, it won't be a matter of maintaining protection or reducing uncertainty; instead, the main focus will be on coping with constant change, and hence with uncertainty. The pressures of turbochange will be overwhelming if the union is constantly on the defense. If the EU is preoccupied with trying to slow change, it will fall behind—in terms of its economy, its human capital, and its entrepreneurial drive. One way or another, the standard European social model must fundamentally change in order for the continent to thrive in a world of turbochange. As Alesina and Giavazzi have argued, vested interests in most European countries still have a firm and stifling grip on political decision-making processes. As a European myself, it's hard for me to imagine that this will really change.

From Hero to Zero

With the EU clearly unable to face down these obstacles, and with such countries as India or Russia unable to progress for different reasons, it is China that remains as the sole real competitor for the United States. As far as some are concerned, the die has already been cast. Indian scholar Arvind Subramanian, who is a chief economic advisor to the Indian government and was formerly a researcher at the IMF, has described a future in which the world in general and the United States in particular need to prepare for "living in the shadow of China's economic dominance."[512] Martin Jacques, a British writer and political scientist, has pushed the argument even further:

> It's banal...to believe that China's influence on the world will be mainly and overwhelmingly economic; on the contrary, its political and cultural effects are likely to be at least as far-reaching.... China's impact on the world will be as great as that of the United States over the last century, probably far greater, and certainly very different....[513]

American foreign policy specialist Stefan Halper leaves little room for doubt. He describes "China's authoritarian model [that] will dominate the twenty-first century" as the "Beijing Consensus."[514] In 2009, then British Foreign Secretary David Miliband described China as the new "indispensable power"—and he was paraphrasing former US Secretary of State Madeleine Albright.[515]

However, a few analysts and observers see China's future in a fundamentally different way. You can find articles with titles like "Why the US, Not China, Will Rule the 21st Century" or "5 Reasons China Won't Take Over the World" all over the place in the blogosphere. Canadian writer Troy Parfitt, who has traveled extensively in China, wrote a popular book entitled "Why China Will Never Rule the World."[516] .

The inner circles of power in China itself have yielded similar sentiments. In early 2013, former Chinese premier Wen Jiabao described the Chinese economy as "unbalanced, un-coordinated, and unsustainable."[517] Mao Yushi, the elderly Chinese economist considered to be one of the main intellectual forces behind Deng Xiaoping's modernization movement, claimed in 2014 that "China is big, but not strong."[518]

In the same year, *The Economist* concluded that as far as foreign investors are concerned, "the golden years are over" for the Chinese economy.[519] Michael Beckley, political scientist at Tufts University, holds very real doubts that the 21st century will be China's century, arguing that "America's edge will endure."[520] Jonathan Fenby, managing director of the Chinese team at the research and consultancy firm Trusted Sources, has also questioned whether Chinese dominance will ever become a reality.[521] Michael Pettis, professor of finance at Peking University's Guanghua School of Management, has seen many reasons to doubt China's possibilities to come to worldwide economic dominance.[522]

But even if China does end up dominating the world economy, Robert Kagan has written that it would still be highly "problematic for China to become a superpower in the geostrategic sense."[523] David Shambaugh, a China specialist and professor of political science and international affairs at George Washington University, defined China as "the partial power" in the sense that "China is not as important, and it is certainly not as influential as conventional wisdom holds."[524] Minxei Pei, a professor of political science at Claremont McKenna College, concluded, "It's not that China doesn't want to be a superpower. The simple truth is that it is not, and will not be one."[525]

Chinese venture capitalist and political scientist Eric Li has written extensively about the "imminent collapse" school on China.[526] In a best-selling book entitled "The Coming Collapse of China," a Chinese attorney educated in the United States by the name of Gordon Chang predicted exactly that. Chang argued that

> on paper, China looks powerful and dynamic.... In reality, however, the Middle Kingdom, as it once called itself, is a paper dragon. Peer beneath the surface, and there is a weak China, one that is in long-term decline and even on the verge of collapse.... Can China's leaders prevent the economic tragedy that is unfolding? The central government is now doing the only thing it can: keeping the economy going through fiscal stimulus on a massive scale...Beijing has about five years to put things right....[527]

So the reality of China's power is subject to widely different interpretations and predictions, but one thing seems to be universally true: Many politicians, analysts, businessmen, and even ordinary citizens in the United States are worried about the rise of China.[528] To gain further insights about China's future, it seems that the long-term historical development China went through would be an excellent starting point. On the basis of meticulously assembled data, historian Angus Maddison has established that in the 10th century, China was the leading economy in the world:

> It outperformed Europe in levels of technology, the intensity with which it used its natural resources and its capacity for administering a huge territorial empire....

> The bureaucracy was the main instrument for impos-
> ing social and political order in a unitary state over a
> huge area.... The economic impact of the bureaucracy
> was very positive for agriculture.... [However,] outside
> agriculture, China's bureaucratic system hindered the
> emergence of an independent commercial and indus-
> trial bourgeoisie on the European pattern. The bureau-
> cracy and gentry of imperial China were quintessential
> rent-seekers.... Entrepreneurial activity was insecure in
> a framework where legal protection for private activity
> was exiguous. Any activity which promised to be lu-
> crative was subject to bureaucratic squeeze.... Interna-
> tional trade and intellectual contacts were severely re-
> stricted. This self-imposed isolation was also a barrier
> to growth.[529]

Not surprisingly, given Maddison's analysis, China began to
gradually lose its lead. Nonetheless, as late as 1820, it still was by
far the largest economy of the world, representing an estimated 33
percent of that world economy.

And yet by 1952, China's share of the world economy had
dropped like a stone to a mere 5.2 percent. Between 1820 and
1952, world per capita income rose threefold, American per capita
income rose ninefold, European per capita income rose fourfold,
and Japanese per capita income rose threefold—and Chinese per
capita income fell. The Renaissance, the Age of Enlightenment,
and the first Industrial Revolution led Western countries forward
in a way never seen before. At the same time, China was isolated
and unable to follow. Its situation was worsened by foreign and
civil wars, natural disasters, internal strife, and ineffective government.

The establishment of Chairman Mao Zedong's communist
People's Republic accelerated China's pace of economic growth via
enforced industrialization. But productivity remained extremely
low. As innovations and productivity grew in the Western world,

Mao's China kept falling behind. By the end of the 1970s, its share of the world economy fell to below 5 percent. Maddison concluded,

> Economic development was interrupted by major political upheavals. There were changes in property rights, the Korean War, the disruption caused by the Sino–Soviet split, the self-inflicted wounds of the Great Leap Forward and the Cultural Revolution.... China was isolated from the booming world economy.... Resources were allocated by government directives and regulation. Market forces played a negligible role.[530]

The bottom line: Mao's communist regime was dictatorial, highly repressive, and murderous,[531] and it also created a hugely inefficient economic system that left the vast majority of the Chinese people very poor and very frightened. By the end of the 1970s, China was a less developed country in every sense of the word, as its per capita income was 1/40 of America's and 1/10 of Brazil's.[532]

Back in Business, but...

After Mao came Deng Xiaoping (1904–1997), who in 1978 initiated a break with the country's disastrous communist history. To Deng and his supporters, it was clear that Mao's regime was about to implode. Deng engaged in a ferocious power struggle with the ultra-extremist Gang of Four, which was led by Jiang Qing, Mao's widow. The Gang of Four wanted to prolong the madness of the Cultural Revolution, but eventually Deng gained the upper hand. The challenge for Deng's camp: Coming up with reforms that would redesign the economic system in ways that production would significantly increase without endangering the absolute political supremacy of China's Communist Party. At the end of 1978, the party's leadership decided that economic progress, rather than class struggle, would henceforth be communist China's main objective.

Deng proceeded carefully in order to not offend the hard-liners who remained inside the party and the army, gradually reintroducing liberalization of agriculture, limited private property rights, some degrees of freedom for profit-oriented entrepreneurship, free markets, and openness to international trade and investment. Following the lead of other Asian countries like Japan, Taiwan, and South Korea, Deng's new China had a two-pronged strategy. First, the vast amount of savings held by households and individuals was channeled toward industrial investments. Second, the currency was devalued several times in order to quickly build an export-oriented industrial sector that turned China into the workshop of the world.[533] Of course, in order for this export-based strategy to succeed, the country had to join the World Trade Organization; it finally succeeded in December 2001. This pivotal change led China's share of worldwide merchandise exports to explode, from 2 percent in the early 1990s to 11.5 percent in 2012.

By the start of the 21st century, the policies set in motion by Deng turned China into the second largest economy in the world. It sustained an annual growth rate averaging close to 10 percent until the financial crisis hit.[534] This rapid economic growth was instrumental in pulling more than half of China's impoverished population out of poverty. In 2003, former Pakistani president Pervez Musharraf expressed an opinion shared by many, saying, "China's economic miracle of the last 20 years is the beacon for all developing countries like Pakistan."[535]

China's string of trade surpluses allowed it to build up foreign exchange reserves to the tune of close to $4 trillion by the end of 2014. As early as 2010, China was well integrated into the world economy at large. It is indeed correct, as Henry Kissinger noted, that China was more "a returning power" than "a rising power."[536] In less than 25 years, the country ditched its social and economic backwardness and reclaimed its position as one of the leading economies of the world, one of the most powerful states on earth, and the leading nation in Asia. But the financial crisis of 2008–2009 and the ensuing global economic recession profoundly affected China's economic prospects. Chinese export demand nosedived from an annual growth rate of 28 percent in mid-2008 to a 27 percent annualized contraction by early 2009.[537]

The Chinese government acted quickly, and massive fiscal and monetary stimulus was applied virtually overnight. As a result, debt exploded within the Chinese economy. Between 2008 and 2014, total debt increased from 147 percent of GDP to 255 percent of GDP,[538] the result of what economic researcher Prasenjit Basu described as "by far the largest monetary expansion in history."[539]

The true debt ratio for China is almost certainly higher still, since local authorities channel a great deal of their investment spending through special investment entities.[540] The Chinese overall debt ratio is close to the average total debt ratio for advanced countries, which stood at the end of 2014 at 279 percent of GDP. The average among the 17 most important emerging countries was almost half the average among advanced countries: 157 percent of GDP at the end of 2014. China lies far above this average and way out in front of countries like Indonesia (66 percent), Russia (85 percent), India (119 percent), and Brazil (142 percent).[541] Debt among central and local authorities in China stands officially at 45 percent of GDP, but if one takes into account off-balance-sheet liabilities, total government debt rises to 55 percent.

But first and foremost, private debt escalated in the wake of the financial crisis, from 117 percent of GDP to close to 200 percent of GDP over the same period (2008–2014). A substantial part of that debt is held in a shadow banking system that almost completely escapes normal regulatory and supervisory procedures and tends to channel credit toward higher-risk borrowers. Shadow banking has mushroomed in China each time authorities have attempted to rein in lending in the official banking sector. Most of Chinese private debt is held by companies, especially state-owned enterprises and property developers. Despite this run-up in debts, economic growth declined substantially, from 10.4 percent in 2010 to 7 percent in 2014.

The Chinese government took such prompt budgetary and monetary action to keep the economy going because of its fear of placing the implicit contract that underlies Chinese society in jeopardy—a contract with Confucian roots. In its most basic form, this contract between China's communist rulers and its population implies that the latter accept limitations on personal freedom and democratic rights in exchange of the former's provision of sufficient jobs and public welfare. For the continuing autocratic rule of the communist party to remain legitimate, those rulers must bring about social and economic progress. According to Stefan Halper, "stability at home...depends on feeding the beast of high-rate economic growth, year upon year."[542]

The ruling elite in Beijing considers 7 percent annual real growth to be the minimum rate required to be able to honor that contract. If it fails to achieve that level of growth, social unrest and political upheaval could result. Core to the Confucian tradition I mentioned is that China's leadership has a responsibility to protect and support, and its people have a duty to obey. When large segments of the population reach higher income levels, how strong will this Confucian tradition be? It certainly seems to be the consensus of China's leadership that if they can't hold their part of the bargain—more growth, more jobs—they will be in trouble, big trouble. Hence, everything possible will be done to avoid such a disaster.

Zombification

In the book *This Time Is Different: Eight Centuries of Financial Folly,* Harvard's Kenneth Rogoff and Carmen Reinhart of the University of Maryland found that almost all financial crises are preceded by exorbitant rises in borrowing and debt buildup.[543] In recent times, South American countries experienced it during the 1980s; Japan in the early 1990s; Indonesia, South Korea, and other emerging countries in the late 1990s; and the United States, Great Britain, Spain, Ireland, and Greece in the mother of all financial crises in 2008–2009. And now China's private sector is leveraged to the hilt and experiencing nominal growth, nosediving from, on average, 15 percent during the first decade of the 21st century to hardly 8 percent in early 2015.

Irving Fisher's by now solidly tested debt deflation theory[544] has proven that when there is lower nominal growth, debtors have much more trouble honoring their debt obligations. This sets in motion a downward spiral throughout the entire economy. Many analysts agree that for China, some form of severe financial crisis is just about a sure thing—along with all the risks that entails for the real economy. Extensive historical data on financial crises and their aftermath have shown that such a crisis would considerably increase public debt as well. Many believe that China's will rise to somewhere between 90 percent and 100 percent of GDP.[545] Such a rise would mean that Chinese public debt wouldn't be much different from that in America or, for that matter, from those in many European nations.[546] It's not a stretch to say that the United States already had its major financial crisis, and the Chinese one is still in the works.

Does the frantic borrowing and the accompanying debt build-up that has characterized China since the financial crisis of 2008–2009 mean a Lehman Brothers–like financial collapse is inevitable? The short answer is no, not least because China's currency is not convertible, and hence an international run on it is not possible.

But that doesn't settle the matter—far from it. The fact that a sudden and chaotic financial crisis probably won't happen does little to mitigate the consequences to Chinese society. I believe that once China is confronted with a truly threatening financial crisis, it will go the Japanese route and choose complacency. The Chinese government will be completely preoccupied with minding the political imperative that economic growth must stay at a certain level to keep public unrest at bay. As a result, too little will be done at the beginning of the crisis to fix the financial system and curb the excesses that invariably arise in the real sector of the economy (overcapacities in some industrial sectors, huge numbers of unsold houses and apartments, useless public works...).[547] Just as in Japan after the credit bubble burst in the early 1990s, zombie companies will be kept alive by credit injections from zombie banks. Every time economic growth dips, the policy elite's first and second impulses will be to provide additional budgetary and/or monetary stimulus.

Increasing the likelihood of this scenario is the availability of ample financial reserves. This will likely push Chinese leadership to continue the status quo in the hope that things will sort themselves out without an avalanche of bankruptcies and job losses. But even in China, the basic laws of economics will prevail. As *The Economist* put it: "Even China cannot cover losses for ever."[548] One way or another, Fisher's vicious debt-deflation mechanism will become a harsh reality.[549]

Markets must be allowed to clean up the mess created by years of frenzied credit and debt expansion—inefficient companies, nonperforming loans, banks with hidden losses, and implicit or explicit continuous bailouts. If not, the mess will keep piling up and will suffocate fresh initiatives and new entrepreneurial ventures. The official count of nonperforming loans at Chinese banks stood at $125 billion at the end of the third quarter of 2014. That "official" figure is considered to be a massive underestimation of the real total.[550] China will not collapse; instead, it will zombify. Gradually, but inevitably, zombification of the economy will spread. Growth will disappear and the risk of deflation will set in, making high debt levels increasingly difficult to manage.

Zombification of the Chinese economy will only reinforce the fundamental shortcomings of the Chinese growth model in place since 1978. According to Keyu Jin, a Chinese professor of economics at the London School of Economics, China's economy is trapped in a "vicious growth cycle."[551] This growth cycle, according to Nobel Prize–winning economist Paul Krugman, will inevitably lead to the model hitting "its Chinese wall, and the only question now is just how bad the crash will be."[552]

China's rapid industrialization was driven by financial repression, resulting in a 0 percent return after correction for inflation on the massive deposits Chinese citizens have put together. Direct and indirect government subsidies have created massive production capacities in traditional industrial sectors like steel, shipbuilding, chemicals, nonferrous metals, and construction materials, and also in newer industries like carbon fiber, photovoltaics, and wind power. In the wake of the financial crisis of 2008–2009, its buildup to industrial overcapacity became frantic. The overcapacity problem, so Li Xinchuang, a senior executive from the Chinese Iron and Steel Association, is "probably beyond anyone's imagination."[553] Unsurprisingly, overcapacity has reduced the rate of return on investment.[554]

Wage growth and employment must be continuously restricted in order to stay competitive in international markets. There, China is faced with increasingly intense competition from India, Vietnam, Mexico, and some Eastern European countries. While GDP growth has averaged 10 percent annually over the last two decades, employment growth came out below 2 percent. Household income as a share of GDP fell from 70 percent in 1990 to 60 percent in 2010. Keyu Jin adds to the list of problems of China's growth model:

The bias toward manufacturing and export industries leads to a severe misallocation of capital. Less efficient industrial sectors have accumulated significant excess capacity, destabilizing the entire economy, while more productive efficient sectors lack access to the resources they need.[555]

The viciousness of China's economic growth model is not the only structural problem its society and leadership face. I group the other fundamental issues faced by Chinese leadership under five categories: demographics, pollution, corruption, inequality, and internal and external security problems. Other countries face some of these problems too, but China has them all, and they are severe.

Aging and Suffocating

In the 1950s and 1960s, Chinese women were encouraged to bear many children in order to boost the number of workers required for Mao's enforced industrialization program. During the 1970s, this trend was reversed and the notorious one-child policy began. As a result, China now faces the most severe aging population trend in human history.[556] In 1999, the OECD warned that China was facing "a demographic time bomb."[557] *The Economist* defined the demographic perspectives as "China's Achilles Heel" and the country's "deadly point of unseen weakness."[558] The *Financial Times* described demographics as "the ghost at China's third plenum" of the 18th Communist Party of China Central Committee.[559]

Demographers and economists estimate that by 2020, China's elderly population will increase by 60 percent and its working population will decline by 35 percent.[560] Despite recent attempts by Chinese leadership to change the one-child policy, the demographic evolution will weigh heavily on government expenditures and is also a drag on the growth potential of the economy. By 2050, China will have 1.6 active workers for each retiree—a disastrous proportion.[561]

A further wrinkle: China's demographic evolution has also led to sex-selective abortions. The current ratio of 120 boys for every 100 girls is an imbalance that leads to societal tensions. Increased immigration could offer a partial solution, but it has its own troubles. On one hand, China has never been open to immigration and doesn't seem inclined to change. On the other hand, China is not regarded by many as an attractive place to live. Many believe that ultimately, China will grow old before it grows rich.

Compared to China, the demographics of the United States look much healthier.[562] Between 2010 and 2050, the US population is expected to increase by 28 percent, from 312 million to 401 million. At the same time, the Chinese population is expected to essentially remain constant around 1.375 billion. During this same 40-year period, the US median age (the age of a person exactly in the middle of the population distribution) is expected to increase from 37 to 41. In China, the median age during this period will jump from 35 to 46.[563]

By 2050, 18.2 percent of the American population will be younger than 15 years (19.8 in 2010); in China, only 14.7 percent will be in that age group (18.1 percent in 2010). In the same year, the dependency ratio, which is the number of people older than 64 per 100 people of working age, will be 36 percent in the United States (19 percent in 2010) and 39 percent in China (11 percent in 2010). The United States is in a better position to face the aging population crisis because it has a higher fertility rate and a tradition of openness to immigration.

On to pollution, the second element in my threat list. The current pollution crisis in China is the obvious result of frantic industrialization. Nowhere on earth—except maybe in the former Soviet Union and its satellites—has environmental quality been sacrificed in the name of economic growth as in China. Blatant disregard for environmental considerations is particularly pronounced at lower levels of government. For example, air pollution is so bad in much of the country that the term "airpocalypse" is commonplace.[564] In 2012, the Asia Development Bank reported that less than 1 percent of the 500 largest cities in China met air quality standards recommended by the World Health Organization. Chinese CO_2 emissions are expected to equal the levels of the United States and Europe *combined* by 2030.[565]

If such a thing is possible, the water in China is even filthier than the air. In February 2013, China's Geological Survey estimated that 90 percent of all Chinese cities had polluted groundwater; 70 percent had "severely polluted water."[566] According to Sara Hsu, a specialist in Chinese economic development at State University of New York, "dumping of industrial chemicals, agricultural waste, and urban wastewater has contaminated China's water resources such that over half of all rivers in the country are unsafe for human contact."[567] By almost any measure, the United States scores much better than China on pollution and is currently working to improve standards further.[568]

"The Friends and Family Conundrum"

A third fundamental issue: widespread corruption that directly and indirectly places a heavy burden on Chinese society and the economy.[569] Corruption in Chinese society was omnipresent during Mao's reign—and even much earlier—but it is ramping up dramatically.[570] Novelist Murong Xuecun, who has long investigated corruption in his country, summarized the tragedy of corruption in China as follows:

> In today's China, business deals are hardly ever carried out fairly. Mostly it's a matter of who you know, or who you pay off, and then the proceeds are divided up and down the chain of corruption.... [With respect to corruption,] most of us Chinese go from being shocked to being numb.... Until China has a new system based on the rule of law, any anti-corruption-

campaign would be simply for show. And, of course, anti-corruption campaigns are often themselves corrupt.... The leadership in Beijing needs corruption and actually encourages it. Corruption is the lubricant, without which everything would grind to a halt.... Not a single person in China can completely break free from corruption.[571]

"Every Communist Party official should keep in mind that all dirty hands will be caught," remarked China's strongman Xi Jinping as he stressed that fighting corruption is one of the major objectives of his administration.[572] Nevertheless, China has moved in the opposite direction on Transparency International's Corruption Perception Index of about 180 countries. In 2013, China was in 80th place; it slipped to 100th in the 2014 ranking. China is now considered more corrupt than India, Colombia, Egypt, or Liberia. Transparency International's report listed several reasons corruption is worsening in China: a lack of transparency and accountability, the ease with which corruption proceeds can be laundered, and a lack of efficient regulation and reform.[537] Either Xi's plan to fight corruption needs more time to get results, or his efforts are, as Murong implied, corrupt. Too often, anticorruption campaigns simply substitute one elite group for another.

Anticorruption campaigns are easily perverted in China because of what's known as the "friends and family conundrum." Any serious reform aimed at fighting corruption "would necessarily undermine one or several levers of elite control, wealth extraction, or both."[574] Stories about wealth accumulation by the political elite are everywhere. Former prime minister Wen Jiabao and his family control close to $3 billion in assets.[575] The Global Financial Integrity network estimated that between 2001 and 2010, China was by far the world's largest source of illicit capital outflows, at $3.8 trillion.[576]

The friends and family conundrum also helps explain why foreign companies and investors receive considerably more harassment about pricing policies and product quality than local companies.[577] Foreign investors also fight constant battles over protection of intellectual property rights, and the Chinese judicial system makes it tough for them to defend themselves. Despite rhetoric to the contrary, the absence of rule of law in China seems to be getting worse instead of better.

Corruption also contributes to the acceleration of income inequality in China. Data compiled by five universities in China and the University of Michigan indicate that inequality in China has risen considerably since 1980. The metric used, the Gini coefficient, measures inequality on a scale from 0 to 1—the higher the Gini coefficient, the higher the inequality. Between 1980 and 2010, China's Gini coefficient has risen from 0.30 to 0.55. In 2010, America's Gini coefficient stood at 0.45.[578] According to a report by Capgemini and RBC Wealth Management, China is now minting more millionaires than any other emerging economy.[579]

Yet the Chinese people are more worried and angry about corruption than about income inequality.[580] The simple truth: Both are inexorably tied together. Public awareness of rampant government corruption combined with record levels of income inequality is a cocktail that easily leads to social unrest.

Threats Everywhere

China also faces countless security issues—internally as well as externally. The chief internal security problems are social unrest and the elite's fear of separatism (known by the Chinese word *fen lie*, or "splittism"). Social unrest is clearly on the rise: The number of "mass incidents," or public gatherings or protests involving more than 100 people, increased from 32,000 in 1999 to 180,000 in 2010—on average, 500 incidents *per day*.[581] Environmental concerns, labor disputes, and improper law enforcement are the major reasons for these actions. Social unrest will climb as economic growth further slows. Chinese citizens will eventually conclude that their leaders are no longer capable of delivering the goods, services, and jobs that constitute their part of the implicit social contract. A rising sense of discontent with pollution, quality of life, corruption, and income inequality will only make things worse.

Separatism is another matter entirely. Xinjiang is a northwestern province in China where the Uighurs, a traditionally Muslim ethnic majority, are seeking greater regional autonomy. Some extreme factions in Xinjiang have resorted to terrorist attacks, and China's leadership is willing to fight tooth and nail against the "three forces" at work there: religious extremism, ethnic separatism, and terrorism. In addition to their desire to quell uprisings there, they are also sensitive to the fact that other Chinese provinces have minority Muslim populations, and they fear that the same sort of extremism may occur there too.

Even more worrisome for Beijing are the 5 million Tibetans who seek greater autonomy. The Tibet issue is extremely sensitive, particularly because of the high international profile of the Tibetans' charismatic spiritual leader, the Dalai Lama.

Taiwan poses both an internal and external security issue for Beijing. Mainland China sees Taiwan as a renegade province that one day must rejoin the mother country. The United States and many other countries see Taiwan as an independent country that should be left alone. A fragile diplomatic truce is currently in place: The United States and China have agreed on the idea of "one China," and China has promised not to force reunification. Over the last two decades, China and Taiwan have forged a very intense financial and economic relationship; hence, a conflict would be detrimental to both sides.

The other external security threat that worries China's leadership is the relative strength of its Asian neighbors, including Taiwan. The United States' neighbors are Canada and Mexico—two countries that are no match for the United States—but China is surrounded by strong, fiercely independent nations like Russia, South Korea, Japan, India, Vietnam, and Australia. Yoon Young-Kwan, a professor at Seoul National University and a former Korean minister of foreign affairs, has written that a fundamental paradox is thwarting the supposed "Asian century." According to him, "deep economic interdependence has done nothing to alleviate strategic mistrust" among the major actors on the Asian continent.[582]

The geographic and geopolitical situation on the Asian continent makes it much

> more problematic for China to become a superpower in the geostrategic sense. That would require something like the collapse of all the other powers in Asia, including India and Japan, and their subservience to Beijing. This would be the equivalent of Moscow's domination of eastern Europe, but much harder to achieve. The Soviet Union wound up dominating eastern Europe because its troops were already in place following the defeat of Germany. China would have to bend its neighbors to its will either without force or through costly war. If it does not, and remains surrounded by these weary great powers, it is hard to see China wielding the kind of global power the Soviet Union did. Even the Soviet Union was not a global superpower in the way the United States was and is, partly because unlike the United States it was surrounded by other great powers.[583]

The United States indirectly plays a role in these politics. Countries like India, Japan, South Korea, Australia, New Zealand, and even Vietnam are strengthening their military and other ties with America in an effort to constrain China's increasing territorial aggressiveness.[584] As the Americans ally with their Asian neighbors, China's leaders have complained that they face a wall of containment. Hu Jintao, China's president from 2003 to 2013, once remarked that the United States

> has strengthened its military deployments in the Asia-Pacific region, strengthened the US–Japan military alliance, strengthened strategic cooperation with India, improved relations with Vietnam, inveighed Pakistan, established a pro-American government in Afghanistan, increased arms sales to Taiwan, and so on. They have extended outposts and placed pressure points on us from the east, south, and west.[585]

Fear, Crippling Fear

What conclusions can be drawn from all this? Since 1978, China has become an economic powerhouse. Continuous strong economic growth made it possible for the communist leadership in Beijing to hold on to its political monopoly. But major cracks in the investment- and export-led economic growth model have rattled the fragile equilibria of China's society and led observers to question its sustainability. Add to this the country's five structural problems—demographics, pollution, corruption, income inequality, and internal and external security threats—and the political leadership has reason for concern.

Now consider turbochange. As turbochange becomes increasingly real and inescapable, the necessity to allow change to take place *hic et nunc* rises disproportionately. That is terrifying to China's leadership. The more uncertainty there is, the more uncontrollable change must be allowed—and the more China's leadership will be crippled by fear. Beijing will increasingly fear losing control of the economy and society.

Most of all, it will fear that its loss of control will lead to chaos, and that chaos will destroy the existing power structures. It's hard not to see similarities to the Soviet Union's attempts to relax autocratic political control and the more recent Arab Spring experiences, where uprisings have led to ungovernable disarray in some nations. That's the kind of evolution the Chinese elite will try to avoid at all cost. At the height of recent democratic demonstrations in Hong Kong, *The Economist* concluded,

> Xi Jinping, China's president, and his colleagues believe that the party's control over the country is the only way of guaranteeing its stability. They fear that if the party loosens its grip, the country will slip toward disorder and disaster....
>
> [There is] a long-standing unwillingness to engage with democrats.[586]

Chinese leaders think about these issues in a highly polarized way; they see no middle ground between strict control and chaos. Whatever the source of unrest may be, the party will first react by tightening its grip on Chinese society.

Pressure from turbochange will force Beijing to make a choice between allowing uncertainty and change to run their course or holding them back by intensifying its grip on Chinese society. The latter is much more likely than the former. This fear of the unknown and of what increased uncertainty and accelerated change will bring will reinforce the desire to keep the status quo. Change will be perceived as an imminent danger to the ruling elite's power, wealth, and influence, and modern-day China has no mechanisms to break up power in a democratic and peaceful way. Creative destruction will not be allowed to run its course.[587] If turbochange takes place at the speed and intensity that I expect it will, America's dominance will be assured.

Epilogue

One More American Revolution

EW IDEAS COME AND GO AS OFTEN AS THE NOTION OF peak oil—the idea that the production of oil, and fossil fuels in general, has reached its zenith and is now on the decline. More often than not, peak oil advocates paint a dark picture of the world's future. At the end of 2013, for example, respected geologist Richard Miller, who once worked for oil titan British Petroleum, predicted that peak oil could be the harbinger of "continuous recession" and that as a result, there will be "more famine, more drought, more resource wars and a steady inflation in the cost of all commodities.... We are probably in peak oil today, or at least in the foot-hills."[588]

Throughout the 20th and the 21st centuries, peak oil pessimists frequently dominated the conversation. In 1909, exactly 50 years after Edwin Drake drilled the first oil well in Venango County, Pennsylvania, it was estimated that the US's "supply [of petroleum] will last about 25 or 30 years."[589] Ten years later, the director of the Bureau of Mines predicted that "in less than 20 years, the supply still underground will be exhausted."[590] Less than 20 years after that, it was estimated that "the present supply [of oil] will last only 15 years."[591]

Marion King Hubbert, an American geoscientist working for the Shell Oil Company, is considered the intellectual father of the notion of peak oil. In 1956, Hubbert predicted that "peak oil production will be reached in the next 10 to 15 years and after that would gradually decline."[592] As time went by, of course, peak oil's date was pushed further back in time. By the late 1970s, the US Department of Energy predicted that peak oil production would come by the early 1990s. Around 2010, peak oil was projected to occur between 2020 and 2030.

What's changed now? New discoveries and the possibility of unconventional sources of oil and gas have increasingly begun to change estimates of exactly how much oil and gas humankind has at its disposal. Proven worldwide oil reserves have increased from 683 billion barrels in 1980 to 1.69 trillion barrels in 2012—an increase due in large part to substantial progress made in deep-sea oil production and in recovery of oil from shale or other "tight rock" formations.[593] This rise in proven reserves took place as oil production increased by almost sixfold over the same period (from 16 million barrels a day to 92 million barrels a day).

Natural gas exploration and production are undergoing a similar change. Former Central Intelligence Agency director John Deutch, who is also a professor of chemistry at MIT, has described the shale revolution as "perhaps the greatest shift in energy estimates in the last half century."[594] Maria van der Hoeven, executive director of the Paris-based International Energy Association (IEA), conceded in May 2013 that "North American supply is an even bigger deal than we thought. A real 'game changer' in every way."[595] This provoked science journalist Charles Mann to ask, "What if we never run out of oil?"[596] The enormous rise in the importance of unconventional sources of oil and gas has fundamentally changed the energy outlook for the United States and the rest of the world, and it's also having a profound impact on political and geostrategic relations.

The United States is playing a crucial role in these new developments. American pioneers and entrepreneurs have found themselves out in front of the rest of the world.[597] The "shale revolution" is caused by technology that allows for recovery of oil and gas from shale rock formation. This recovery takes place via a combination horizontal drilling and hydraulic fracturing ("fracking"), which consists of blasting shale rock formations with a mixture of water, chemicals, and sand, and shale rock is abundant in many American states, including New York, Ohio, West Virginia, Texas, and North Dakota.

In fact, the IEA has determined that the steep increase in shale oil production will lead the United States to overtake Saudi Arabia and Russia as the top oil producer in the world by 2017. And even before that, the United States will also overtake Russia as the number one producer of natural gas in the world. Most energy experts expect the United States to be self-sufficient in energy by the early 2020s.

And the shale revolution is not just bringing back the prospect of energy independence so dear to a majority of American citizens. It's also the root of the country's reindustrialization[598] in such energy-intensive industries as chemicals, petrochemicals, automotive, cement, and steel.

Thus, the shale oil and gas revolution has substantially changed geopolitical positions and relations.[599] Consider, for example, the significance of the OPEC cartel and Saudi Arabia in oil markets, Russia's geostrategic power position, Iran's strategic relevance, and weaknesses in China's economic model. Robin West, energy specialist and CEO of PFC Energy, considers the shale oil and gas developments to be

> the energy equivalent of the Berlin Wall coming down. Just as the trauma of the Cold War ended in Berlin, so the trauma of the 1973 oil embargo is ending now. The

geopolitical implications of this change are striking. We will no longer rely on the Middle East, or compete with such nations as China or India for resources.[600]

According to the British political scientists David Hastings Dunn and Mark McClelland, the shale oil and gas revolution in the United States

> offers a distinct likelihood that the economic foundation underpinning US hegemony is not nearly as fragile as has been argued. While the economic crisis that began in 2008 and the military campaigns in Afghanistan and Iraq have certainly damaged US power, the rapid expansion of the US energy sector suggests that these events are more properly seen as serious temporary setbacks rather than fatal blows to American pre-eminence. Rather like the impact of the Vietnam War and the oil shocks of the 1970s, their impact on the global role of the United States may be less fundamental than contemporary reactions suggest.[601]

Messy and Chaotic, but Working

China, Australia, Africa, Russia, Central Europe, the United Kingdom, and Latin America are also blessed with huge shale rock formations, but the United States has led the shale revolution. In my opinion, this is direct evidence of my thesis that America is best suited to succeed in a world of turbochange.

Turbochange is fueled by the development of and interaction between human capital and knowledge advancement, entrepreneurial drive, and the forces of globalization, and America's unique blend of historical, institutional, and sociological elements supports its feverish quest for perpetual change and its ability to thrive in it. The shale revolution fits the turbochange paradigm almost perfectly. In less than a decade, it has fundamentally changed the worldwide energy situation. That this happened in the United States is not a coincidence.

The British weekly *The Economist* remarked that the firms responsible for the shale oil and gas boom "embody an all-American formula of maverick engineers, bold entrepreneurs and risk hungry capital markets that no country can match."[602] In a similar vein, highly respected energy economist Phil Verleger pointed out that the shale revolution has not resulted from government policies or from big oil companies drilling for new energy resources: "This is really the classic success of American entrepreneurs.... These were people who saw this coming, managed to assemble the capital and go ahead."[603]

The Economist also added an important element to Verleger's emphasis on the entrepreneurial aspects of the shale revolution, noting that the new oil and gas boom that the United States is experiencing

> owes less to geological luck than enterprise, ready finance and dazzling technology. America's energy firms have invested in new ways of pumping out hydrocarbons that everyone knew were there but could not extract economically. The new oilfields in Texas and North Dakota resemble high-tech factories.[604]

It's all there—human capital and knowledge technology, entrepreneurial drive, and globalization. After all, what other market is more internationalized than the fossil fuel market?

Geologists have long been aware that shale rock formations contained huge amounts of natural gas and oil, but profitable production from them was impossible because of the limits of technology. Entrepreneurs such as George Mitchell (1919–2013), an independent natural gas producer working in the huge Barnett Shale formation in northern Texas, ceaselessly searched for new technology to help them extract fossil fuels from shale formations.

Mitchell, who personally spent millions of dollars to solve the problem, wasn't taken seriously by the big players in the oil business, and was often ridiculed.

By the late 1990s, Mitchell's tireless work paid off. He developed a profitable way to extract oil and gas—hydraulic fracturing, or fracking. When Mitchell's technology was combined with horizontal drilling techniques developed by Devon Energy, another major player in the American natural gas market, it was only a matter of time before the right environment would allow the shale revolution to really take off. That happened in 2007 and early 2008, when the oil market tightened dramatically and crude prices per barrel jumped from around $60 to above $100.

America's commitment to individual property rights also greatly supported the shale revolution, as it offers unrivaled protection to investors, innovators, and enterprises. Suddenly, these entrepreneurs and adventurers made the dire predictions about peak oil look foolish. Instead of shooting up to $300 or even $400 per barrel, as some projected, oil prices declined sharply during the latter half of 2014. Energy specialist Daniel Yergin declared the oil age to be far from over, as he believes that around 1 trillion barrels of oil were produced in the past century and that *at least* five trillion barrels of oil are most likely still available. About a third of these five billion barrels are only accessible today because of fracking technology.[605]

The intensity and speed with which this revolution developed was truly amazing. Daring entrepreneurs went all the way, taking enormous risks while developing their ventures. The buildup of debt to finance outlays for equipment, drilling acreage, and related items was breathtaking. Some succeeded, but many lost everything. Between 2004 and 2013, debt among American independent energy companies skyrocketed from $50 billion to $250 billion—quite the "asset bubble." As oil and gas prices fall, as they surely have from mid-2014 through early 2015, bankruptcies and job losses are inevitable.

But we know that technology is a rolling stone. There will be further innovations, and those will reduce the cost of shale oil and gas extraction. As noted by Mark Mills, senior fellow at the Manhattan Institute:

> Among the thousands of shale producers, you can guarantee there are pioneers just like those who started the shale revolution. As profit margins erode due to low or even lower future prices, the pioneers will try out the revolutionary new shale techniques that have yet to be deployed.[606]

This new know-how will also be used in other industries. The shale revolution as we know it today is built on a foundation of computer technologies, drilling techniques, and geophysics. It's hard to imagine that other applications won't follow.

And this is all part of the "American way" of moving a system forward, of bringing about change. It's Joseph Schumpeter's creative destruction in its truest form. For example, the terminals American companies built to import gas into the country made a lot of sense in the period before the shale revolution. Today, those terminals are being adapted for a new purpose in a new reality: exporting low-cost gas produced in the United States.

The process by which changes like this take place often looks chaotic and messy. There will be overinvestment. Money will be wasted. Bubbles will burst. Crashes will follow. The cost to society is often great, but it does eventually work out. Those that succeed thrive and deliver progress to society. Those who fail have many incentives to try again.

Of course, the shale revolution is not proof of continued American dominance in world affairs. Instead, it's a striking example of how, and how well, the American system works. Because the system's processes often look chaotic and messy—and often *are* chaotic and messy—many find them to be dysfunctional, and not worth the heavy cost paid in terms of social and human adjustment. (In the case of the shale revolution, ecological costs are also a significant factor.[607]) But these costs are more easily accepted and assimilated in the United States than in most other countries and cultures.

The problems facing the United States are enormous, including a dysfunctional political system, a mountain of public debt, pervasive income inequality, an ailing infrastructure, weakness among some of America's traditional allies, and growing strength in China and Russia. But Winston Churchill once compared the United States to some "gigantic boiler," quiet and cold until "the fire is lighted under it," and at that point, he believed, there was "no limit to the power it can generate."[608] I completely agree. Turbochange will be the fire needed to get the American boiler going, and it will light the boiler's fire with ever more frequency and intensity.

Bibliography

ABDULKADIROGLU, Atila, ANGRIST, Joshua, COHODES, Sarah, DY-NARSKI, Sue, FULLERTON, Jon, KANE, Tom and PATAK, Parag, 2009, *Informing the Debate: Comparing Boston's Charter, Pilot, and Traditional Schools*, Boston, Boston Foundation

ABRAMOVITZ, Moses, 1952, "Economic Growth," in HALEY, B., *A Survey of Contemporary Economics*, vol. II, Homewood, Ill., Richard D. Irwin

ACEMOGLU, Daron, 1996, "A Microfoundation for Social Increasing Returns in Human Capital Accumulation," *Quarterly Journal of Economics*, August

ACEMOGLU, Daron and AUTOR, David, 2010, "Skills, Tasks, and Technologies: Implications for Employment and Earnings," *NBER working paper*, Cambridge, Mass., National Bureau of Economic Research

ACEMOGLU, Daron and ROBINSON, James, 2012, *Why Nations Fail: The Origins of Power, Prosperity, and Poverty*, New York, Random House

——, 2014, "The Rise and Fall of General Laws of Capitalism," working paper available at http://economics.mit.edu/files/10302 (accessed September 18, 2014)

AJAMI, Fouad, 2003, "The Falseness of Anti-Americanism," *Foreign Policy*, September 1

AKERLOF, George and SHILLER, Robert, 2009, *Animal Spirits. How Human Psychology Drives the Economy, and Why It Matters for Global Capitalism*, Princeton, NJ, Princeton University Press

ALESINA, Alberto and GIAVAZZI, Franceso, 2006, *The Future of Europe: Reform or Decline*, Cambridge, Mass., The MIT Press

ALEXANDER, Charles, 1969, *Nationalism in American Thought, 1930-1945*, Chicago, Rand McNally

AMSDEN, Alice, 2001, *The Rise of "The Rest": Challenges to the West by Late-Industrializing Countries*, New York, Oxford University Press

ANDERSON, Jonathan, 2009, "Beijing's Exceptionalism," *National Interest*, no. 100, March/April

ANNUNZIATA, Marco, GILLANDERS, Hugh, HAENEN, Chris, HEMS-WORTH, Simon and SOLTESZ, J.P., 2014, *The State of European Innovation*, London, General Electric Europe, October

ARROW, Kenneth, 1962(a), "Economic Welfare and the Allocation of Resources for Invention," in *The Rate and Direction of Inventive Activity*, Princeton, NJ, Princeton University Press

———— 1962(b), "The Economic Implications of Learning by Doing," *Review of Economic Studies*, June

ARTHUR, W. Brian, 2009, *The Nature of Technology: What It Is and How It Evolves*, New York, The Free Press

ATKINSON, Richard and BLANPIED, William, 2008, "Research Universities: Core of the US Science and Technology System," *Technology in Society*, no. 30

AUDRETSCH, David, KEILBACH, Max and LEHMAN, Erik, 2006, *Entrepreneurship and Economic Growth*, Oxford, UK, Oxford University Press

AUTEN, Gerald and GEE, Geoffrey, 2009, "Income Mobility in the United States: New Evidence from Income Tax Data," *National Tax Journal*, 62, June

AUTEN, Gerald, GEE, Geoffrey and TURNER, Nicholas, 2013, "New Perspectives on Income Mobility and Inequality," *National Tax Journal*, 66(4), December

BACEVICH, Andrew, 2008, *The Limits of Power: The End of American Exceptionalism*, New York, Metropolitan

BAILY, Martin, MANYIKA, James and GUPTA, Shalab, 2013, "US Productivity Growth: An Optimistic Perspective," *International Productivity Monitor*, Spring

BALL, Philip, 2012, *Why Society Is a Complex Matter*, Berlin, Springer Verlag

BAUDEAU, Nicolas, 1767, *Première Introduction à la Philosophie Economique*, Paris, N. Dubois (edition 1910)

BAUMOL, William, 2002(a), *The Free-Market Innovation Machine: Analyzing the Growth Miracle of Capitalism*, Princeton, NJ, Princeton University Press

———— 2002(b), *Entrepreneurship, Innovation and Growth: The David–Goliath Symbiosis*, mimeo available on Baumol's website at New York University

BAUMOL, William; LITAN, Robert and SCHRAMM, Carl, 2007, *Good Capitalism, Bad Capitalism and the Economics of Growth and Prosperity*, New Haven, Conn., Yale University Press

BECKER, Gary, 1993, *Human Capital: A Theoretical and Empirical Analysis with Special Reference to Education*, Chicago, University of Chicago Press, 3d edition

BECKLEY, Michael, 2011, "China's Century? Why America's Edge Will Endure." *International Security*, 36(3)

BELL, Daniel, 1975, "The End of American Exceptionalism," *The Public Interest*, Fall

BEN-AMI, Shlomo, 2013, "The Rise of an Insecure Giant," *Project Syndicate*, December 3

BENTLEY, Jerry, 1993, *Old World Encounters: Cross-Cultural Contacts and Exchanges in Pre-modern Times*, New York, Oxford University Press

———— 1999, "Asia in World History," *Education about Asia*, 4

BERKOWITZ, Bruce, 2007, "Strategy for a Long Struggle," *Policy Review*, February/March

BHIDÉ, Amar, 2008, *The Venturesome Economy: How Innovation Sustains Prosperity in a More Connected World*, Princeton, NJ, Princeton University Press

BLACK, Jeremy, 2008, *Great Powers and the Quest for Hegemony*, New York, Routledge

BLAINEY, Geoffrey, 1973, *The Causes of War*, New York, The Free Press (edition 1988)

BONGIOVANNI, Francesco, 2012, *The Decline and Fall of Europe*, New York, Palgrave Macmillan

BORDO, Michael, 2002, "Globalization Is Historical Perspective," *Business Economics*, January

BOUDREAUX, Donald and PERRY, Mark, 2013, "The Myth of a Stagnant Middle Class," *Wall Street Journal*, January 23

BRANDON, Henry, 1974, *The Retreat of American Power*, New York, Delta

BRANDS, H.W., 2000, *The First American: The Life and Times of Benjamin Franklin*, New York, Random House

BREINART, Peter, 2014, "The End of American Exceptionalism," *The National Journal*, February 3

BREMMER, Ian, 2010, *The End of the Free Market*, New York, Portfolio, Penguin Group

BROGAN, Denis, 1953, "The Illusion of American Omnipotence" as reprinted in BROGAN, D., 1963, *American Aspects*, London, Hamish Hamilton

BRYCE, James, 1888, *The American Commonwealth*, London, Macmillan (2 vols.)

BRYNJOLFSSON, Eric and McAFEE, Andrew, 2011, *Race against the Machine: How the Digital Revolution Is Accelerating Innovation, Driving Productivity, and Irreversibly Transforming Employment and the Economy*, Lexington, Mass., Digital Frontier Press

————— 2014, *The Second Machine Age. Work Progress, and Prosperity in a Time of Brilliant Technologies*, New York, W.W. Norton

BUCHANAN, Patrick, 1998, *The Great Betrayal: How American Sovereignty and Social Justice Are Being Sacrificed to the Gods of the Global Economy*, New York, Little, Brown

BURTLESS, Gary, 2014, *Income Growth and Income Inequality: The Facts May Surprise You*, Washington, DC, The Brookings Institution, posted on January 6

BUSH, Vannevar, 1945, *Science: The Endless Frontier*, Washington, DC, National Science Foundation (reprinted 1990)

BUTTIGLIONE, Luigi, LANE, Philip, REICHLIN, Lucrezia and REINHART, Vincent, 2014, *Deleveraging? What Deleveraging?* Geneva, International Center for Monetary and Banking Studies, Geneva Reports on the World Economy, no. 16

CALLEO, David, 1992, *The Bankrupting of America: How the Federal Budget Is Impoverishing the Nation*, New York, William Morrow

CAMAROTA, Steven, 2011, *Welfare Use by Immigrant Households with Children*, Backgrounder, Washington, DC, Center for Immigration Studies, April

CAMPBELL-KELLY, Martin and ASPRAY, William, 1996, *Computer: A History of the Information Machine*, New York, Basic Books

CANTILLON, Richard, 1755, *Essai sur la Nature du Commerce en General*, London, Macmillan (edition 1931)

CAPELLI, Peter, 2014, "Skill Gaps, Skill Shortages and Skill Mismatches: Evidence for the US," *NBER working paper series*, Cambridge, Mass., National Bureau of Economic Research, 20382 (August)

CARR, Nicholas, 2011, *The Shallows: What the Internet Is Doing to Our Brain*, New York, Atlantic Books

CARSON, Rachel, 1962, *Silent Spring*, New York, Houghton Mifflin

CEASER, James, 1997, *Reconstructing America: The Symbol of America in Modern Thought*, New Haven, Conn., Yale University Press

————— 2003, "A Genealogy of Anti-Americanism," *Public Interest*, summer

————— 2012, "The Origins and Character of American Exceptionalism," *American Political Thought*, spring

CHANDLER, Alfred, 1977, *The Visible Hand: The Managerial Revolution in American Business*, Cambridge, Mass., Harvard University Press

————— 1990, *Scale and Scope: The Dynamics of Industrial Capitalism*, Cambridge, Mass., Harvard University Press

CHETTY, Raj, FRIEDMAN, John and ROCKOFF, Jonah, 2011, "The Long-Term Impacts of Teachers: Teacher Value-Added and Student Outcomes in Adulthood," *NBER working paper series*, Cambridge, Mass., National Bureau of Economic Research, 17699

CHEVALIER, Michel, 1866, "La Guerre et la crise européenne," *Revue des Deux Mondes*, June 1

CHOROST, Michael, 2011, *World Wide Mind. The Coming Integration of Humanity, Machines, and the Internet*, New York, The Free Press

CHRISTENSEN, Clayton, 1997, *The Innovator's Dilemma: When New Technologies Cause Great Firms to Fail*, Boston, Harvard Business School Press

COASE, Ronald, 1960, "The Problem of Social Cost," *Journal of Law and Economics*, 1

COHEN, Daniel, 2012, *The Prosperity of Vice: A Worried View of Economics*, Cambridge, Mass., The MIT Press

COMPTON, James, 1968, *The Swastika and the Eagle*, New York, Houghton Mifflin

CONRAD, Peter, 2014, *How the World Was Won: The Americanization of Everywhere*, London, Thames & Hudson

COOPER, Richard, 2005, "Whither China?" *Japan Center for Economic Research Bulletin*, September

COWEN, Tyler, 2011, *The Great Stagnation: How America Ate All the Low-Hanging Fruit of Modern History, Got Sick, and Will (Eventually) Feel Better*, New York, Dutton

COX, Michael, 2011, "Power Shift and the Death of the West? Not Yet!" *European Political Science*, 10:3

CRABB, Cecil, 1986, *Policy-Makers and Critics: Conflicting Theories of American Foreign Policy*, New York, Praeger

CRICHTON, Michael, 1992, *Rising Sun*, New York, Alfred A. Knopf

CUKIER, Kenneth and MAYER-SCHOENBERGER, Victor, 2013, *Big Data: A Revolution That Will Transform How We Live*, New York, Houghton, Mifflin, Harcourt

CULLEN, Murphy, 2007, *Are We Rome? The Fall of an Empire and the Fate of America*, Boston, Houghton Mifflin

CUMINGS, Bruce, 2009, *Dominion from Sea to Sea*, New Haven, Conn., Yale University Press

CURDIA, Vasco and FERRERO, Andrea, 2013, "How Stimulatory Are Large-Scale Asset Purchases?" *Economic Letter*, Federal Reserve Bank of San Francisco, August 13

DACHS, Bernhard, STEHRER, Robert and ZAHRADNIK, Georg, 2014, *The Internationalization of Business R&D*, Chattenham, UK, Edward Elgar

DARWIN, Charles, 1845, *Journal of Researches into the Natural History and Geology of the Countries Visited during the Voyage of H.M.S. Beagle around the World*, London

DAWISHA, Karen, 1990, *Eastern Europe, Gorbachev, and Reform: The Great Challenge*, Cambridge, UK, Cambridge University Press

de MONTHERLANT, Henry, 1963, *"Le Chaos" et "La Nuit,"* Paris, Gallimard

de PAUW, Cornelius, 1770, *Recherches philosophiques sur les Américains. Mémoires intéressants pour server à l'histoire de l'espèce humaine*, 3 vols., Upper Saddle River, NJ, Gregg Press (edition 1968)

de TOCQUEVILLE, Alexis, 1835–40, *Democracy in America*, Chicago, University of Chicago Press (edition 2000)

DeLONG, James, 2012, *America's Crisis of Political Legitimacy*, Washington, DC, American Enterprise Institute

DER SPIEGEL, 2010, "Superpower in Decline," *Spiegelonline*, January 11

DEUTCH, John, 2011, "The Good News about Gas," *Foreign Affairs*, 90:1

DOWD, Alan, 2007, "Three Centuries of Declinism," www.realclearpolitics.com/articles/2007/08/declinism.html, August

DRUCKER, Peter, 1985, *Innovation and Entrepreneurship: Practice and Principles*, New York, Harper & Row

DYER, Geoff, 2014, *The Contest of the Century: The New Era of Competition with China—And How America Can Win*, New York, Alfred A. Knopf

EASTERBROOK, Gregg, 2009, *Sonic Boom: Globalization at Mach Speed*, New York, Random House

ECKES, Alfred, 1995, *Opening America's Market: US Foreign Trade Policy since 1776*, Chapel Hill, NC, University of North Carolina Press

EHRLICH, Isaac, 2007, "The Mystery of Human Capital as Engine of Growth; or, Why the US Became the Economic Superpower in the Twentieth Century," *NBER working paper series*, Cambridge, Mass., National Bureau of Economic Research, 12868 (January)

EICHENGREEN, Barry, 2011, *Exorbitant Privilege: The Rise and Fall of the Dollar and the Future of the International Monetary System*, Oxford, UK, Oxford University Press

ELLUL, Jacques, 1964, *The Technological Society*, New York, Random House

EMMOTT, Bill, 2008, *Rivals: How the Power Struggle Between China, India, and Japan Will Shape Our Next Decade*, Orlando, Harcourt

———— 2012, "The American Century Is Not Over," *Prospect*, December

ESLER, Gavin, 1998, *The United States of Anger*, London, Penguin Books

EVANS, Michael, 2011, "Power and Paradox: Asian Geopolitics and Sino-American Relations in the 21st Century," *Orbis*, 55:1

EWING, Walter, 2012, *Opportunity and Exclusion. A Brief of US Immigration Policy*, Washington, DC, The Immigration Policy Center

FALLOWS, James, 1989, "Containing Japan," *Atlantic Monthly*, May

FENBY, Jonathan, 2014, *Will China Dominate the 21st Century?* New York, John Wiley

FERGUSON, Niall, 2004, *Colossus. The Rise and Fall of the American Empire*, New York, Penguin Books (paperback edition, 2005)

—— 2010, "Decline and Fall: When the American Empire Goes, It Is Likely to Go Quickly," *Foreign Affairs*, March/April

FINDLAY, Ronald and O'ROURKE, Kevin, 2008, *Power and Plenty: Trade, War, and the World Economy in the Second Millenium*, Princeton, NJ, Princeton University Press

FISHER, Irving, 1933, "The Debt-Deflation Theory of Great Depressions," *Econometrica*, 1(4)

FITZ, Marshall, WOLGIN, Philip and OAKFORD, Patrick, 2013, *Immigrants Are Makers, Not Takers*, Washington, DC, Center for American Progress, February 8

FLETCHER, Ian, 2010, *Free Trade Doesn't Work: What Should Replace It and Why*, Washington, DC, U.S. Business and Industry Council

FLYNN, Stephen, 2008, "America the Resilient," *Foreign Affairs*, March/April

FONER, Eric, 2002, *Reconstruction: America's Unfinished Revolution 1863-1877*, New York, HarperCollins

FORBES, Jack, 1968, "Frontiers in American History and the Role of the Frontier Historian," *Ethnohistory*, 15(2)

FRANK, Andre Gunder, 1998, *ReOrient: Global Economy in the Asian Age*, Berkeley, Calif., University of California Press

FRANK, Andre Gunder and GILLS, Barry, eds., 1993, *The World System: Five Hundred or Five Thousand Years?* London, Routledge

FRANK, Robert and COOK, Philip, 1996, *The Winner-Take-All-Society: Why the Few at the Top Get So Much More than the Rest of Us*, New York, Penguin Books

FRIEDMAN, Milton, 1989, *The Crime of 1873*, Hoover Institution, Stanford University, working papers in economics E-89-12

FRIEDMAN, Milton and SCHWARTZ, Anna, 1963, *A Monetary History of the United States, 1867-1960*, Princeton, NJ, Princeton University Press

FRIEDMAN, Thomas, 2005, "It's a Flat World, After All," *New York Times Magazine*, April 3

FUKUYAMA, Francis, 1989, "The End of History?" *The National Interest*, summer

———— 1992, *The End of History and the Last Man*, New York, The Free Press

———— 2014, "America in Decay: The Sources of Political Dysfunction," *Foreign Affairs*, September/October

FURSENKO, Aleksandr and NAFTALI, Timothy, 1997, *One Hell of a Gamble: Khrushchev, Castro, Kennedy and the Cuban Missile Crisis, 1958-1964*, New York, W.W. Norton & Company

GADDIS, John Lewis, 1997, *We Now Know: Rethinking Cold War History*, Oxford, UK, Oxford University Press

GAI, Prasanna and KAPADIA, Sujit, 2010, "Contagion in Financial Networks," *Proceedings of the Royal Society*, 466(2120)

GALAMA, Titus and HOSEK, James, 2008, *US Competitiveness in Science and Technology*, Santa Monica, Calif., RAND Corporation

GALBRAITH, John, 1956, *American Capitalism*, Boston, Houghton Mifflin

GARWIN, Laura and LINCOLN, Tim, eds., 2003, *A Century of Nature: Twenty-one Discoveries That Changed Science and the World*, Chicago, University of Chicago Press

GERBI, Antonello, 1973, *The Dispute of the New World: The History of a Polemic, 1750-1990*, Pittsburgh, University of Pittsburgh Press

GERSCHENKRON, Alexander, 1962, *Economic Backwardness in Historical Perspective*, Cambridge, Mass., Harvard University Press

GILPIN, Robert, 1975, *US Power and the Multinational Corporation: The Political Economy of Foreign Direct Investment*, New York, Basic Books

———— 1981, *War and Change in World Politics*, Cambridge, UK, Cambridge University Press

GINGRICH, Newt, 2011, *A Nation Like No Other: Why American Exceptionalism Matters*, Washington, DC, Regnery Publishing

GLAESER, Edward, 2011, *The Triumph of the City: How Our Greatest Invention Makes US Richer, Smarter, Greener, Healthier, and Happier*, New York, Penguin Press

GLAESER, Edward, PONZETTO, Giacomo and SHLEIFER, Andrei, 2007, "Why Does Democracy Need Education," *Journal of Economic Growth* 12(2)

GLASNER, David and COOLEY, Thomas, 1997, *Business Cycles and Depressions*, New York, Garland Publishing

GORDON, Colin, 2013, *Growing Apart: A Political History of American Inequality*, Washington, DC, Institute for Policy Studies

GORDON, Robert, 2012, "Is US Economic Growth Over? Faltering Innovation Confronts Six Headwinds," *NBER working paper series*, Cambridge, Mass., National Bureau of Economic Research, 18315 (August)

GRANOVETTER, Mark, 1985, "Economic Action and Social Structure: The Problem of Embeddedness," *American Journal of Sociology*, 91(3)

GREEN, Stephen, 2014, "China—Total Debt Breaks 250% of GDP," *Standard Chartered Bank Research*, London, July

GREGG, Samuel, 2013, *Becoming Europe: Economic Decline, Culture, and How America Can Avoid a European Future*, New York, Encounter Books

GRILICHES, Zvi, 1957, "Hybrid Corn: An Exploration in Economics of Technological Change," *Econometrica*, October

———— 1979, "Issues in Assessing the Contribution of Research and Development to Productivity Growth," *Bell Journal of Economics*, 10

GROS, Daniel, 2014, "The Transatlantic Growth Gap," *CEPS Commentary*, Centre for European Policy Studies, August 5

GROSS, Daniel, 2012, *Better, Stronger, Faster: The Myth of American Decline...and the Rise of a New Economy*, New York, The Free Press

HAASS, Richard, 2013, *Foreign Policy Begins at Home: The Case for Putting America's House in Order*, New York, Basic Books

HALDANE, Andrew, 2013, "Why Institutions Matter (More than Ever)," speech given at the *Centre for Research on Socio-Cultural Change (CRESC)*, Annual Conference, London, September 4

HALPER, Stefan, 2010, *The Beijing Consensus: How China's Authoritarian Model Will Dominate the Twenty-first Century*, New York, Basic Books

HANSEN, Paul and KNOWLES, Stephen, 1998, "Human Capital and Returns to Scale," *Journal of Economic Studies*, 25(2)

HARFORD, Tim, 2014, "Big Data: Are We Making a Big Mistake?" *Financial Times*, March 28

HARRINGTON, Michael, 1963, *The Other America: Poverty in the United States*, Baltimore, Penguin

HASTINGS DUNN, David and McCLELLAND, Mark, 2013, "Shale Gas and the Revival of American Power: Debunking Decline?" *International Affairs*, 89

HAYNES, Sam and MORRIS, Christopher, eds., 1997, *Manifest Destiny and Empire: American Antebellium Expansionism*, College Station, Texas, Texas A&M University Press

HECK, Stefan and ROGERS, Matt (with CARROLL, Paul), 2014, *Resource Revolution: How to Capture the Biggest Business Opportunity in a Century*, New York, Melcher Media

HEIDEGGER, Martin, 1953, "The Question Concerning Technology," as reprinted in KRELL, David Farrell, ed., 1992, *Martin Heidegger. Basic Writings: From "Being and Time" (1927) to "The Task of Thinking" (1964)*, San Francisco, Harper

HELD, David, McGREW, Anthony, GOLDBLATT, David and PERRATON, Jonathan, 1999, *Global Transformations: Politics, Economics, and Culture*, Stanford, Calif., Stanford University Press

HEWITT, Gavin, 2013, *The Lost Continent*, London, Hodder & Stoughton

HILL, Steven, 2010, *Europe's Promise: Why the European Way Is the Best Hope in an Insecure Age*, Berkeley, Calif., University of California Press

HIRSCHMAN, Albert, 1958, *The Strategy of Economic Development*, New Haven, Conn., Yale University Press

HODGSON, Godfrey, 2009, *The Myth of American Exceptionalism*, New Haven, Conn., Yale University Press

HOFFMAN, Daniel, 1999, *Paul Bunyan: Last of the Frontier Demigods*, Lansing, Mich., Michigan State University Press

HOFFMAN, David and POLK, Andrew, 2014, *The Long Soft Fall in Chinese Growth*, New York, The Conference Board

HSU, Sara, 2013, "China's Water Pollution Mire," *The Diplomat*, May 28

HUANG, Yasheng, 2008, *Capitalism with Chinese Characteristics: Entrepreneurship and the State*, New York, Cambridge University Press

HUESEMANN, Michael and HUESEMANN, Joyce, 2011, *Technofix: Why Technology Won't Save Us or the Environment*, Gabriola Island, Canada, New Society Publishers

HUNTINGTON, Samuel, 1988, "The US—Decline or Renewal?" *Foreign Affairs*, winter

——— 1999, "The Lonely Superpower," *Foreign Affairs*, March/April

HYMAN, Louis, 2012, *Debtor Nation: The History of America in Red Ink*, Princeton, NJ, Princeton University Press

IGNATIEFF, Michael, 2014, "We Need a New Bismarck to Tame the Machines," *Financial Times*, February 10

IKENBERRY, John, ed., 2002, *America Unrivaled: The Future of the Balance of Power*, Ithaca, NY, Cornell University Press

ISENBERG, Daniel, 2013, *Worthless, Impossible, and Stupid. How Contrarian Entrepreneurs Create and Capture Extraordinary Value*, Boston, Harvard Business Review Press

JACOBS, Jane, 1969, *The Economy of Cities*, New York, Random House

JACQUES, Martin, 2009, *When China Rules the World: The End of the Western World and the Birth of New Global Order*, London, Allen Lane

JAMES, Harold, 2009, *The Creation and Destruction of Value: The Globalization Cycle*, Cambridge, Mass., Harvard University Press

JIN, Keyu, 2014, "China's Vicious Growth Circle," *Project Syndicate*, October 16

JOFFE, Josef, 2014, *The Myth of America's Decline: Politics, Economics, and a Half Century of False Prophecies*, New York, W.W. Norton & Company

JONES, Charles, 2005, "Growth and Ideas," in AGHION, P. and DURLAUF, S., *Handbook of Economic Growth*, Amsterdam, Elsevier New Holland

JONES, Ernest, 1961, *The Life and Work of Sigmund Freud*, New York, Basic Books

JONES, Steve, 2006, *Against Technology: From the Luddites to Neo-Luddism*, New York, Routledge

JORGENSON, Dale and FRAUMENI, Barbara, 1989, "The Accumulation of Human and Non-human Capital, 1948-84," in *The Measurement of Saving, Investment, and Wealth*, Chicago, University of Chicago Press for National Bureau of Economic Research

JUN, Zhang, 2014, "China's Growth Secret," *Project Syndicate*, December 26

KAGAN, Robert, 2012, *The World America Made*, New York, Alfred A. Knopf

KAHNEMAN, Daniel, 2011, *Thinking, Fast and Slow*, New York, Farrar, Straus and Giroux

KAMMEN, Michael, ed., 1986, *The Origins of the American Constitution: A Documentary History*, New York, Viking Penguin Books

KAPLAN, Steven and RAUH, Joshua, 2013, "It's the Market: The Broad-Based Rise in the Return to Top Talent," *Journal of Economic Perspectives*, 27(3)

KARNOW, Stanley, 1994, *Vietnam: A History*, London, Penguin Books

KASPAROV, Garry, LEVCHIN, Max and THIEL, Peter, 2012, *The Blueprint: Reviving Innovation, Rediscovering Risk, and Rescuing the Free Market*, New York, W.W. Norton

KEESING, Donald, 1966, "Labor Skills and Comparative Advantage," *American Economic Review*, 56

KENNEDY, Paul, 1987, *The Rise and Fall of the Great Powers*, New York, Random House

———— 2002(a), "The Eagle Has Landed," *Financial Times*, February 2

———— 2002(b), "Power and Terror," *Financial Times*, September 3

KETS de VRIES, Manfred, 1977, "The Entrepreneurial Personality: A Person at the Crossroads," *Journal of Management Studies*, vol. 14

KEYNES, John Maynard, 1919, *The Economic Consequences of the Peace*, as available online at socser2.socsci.mcmaster.ca/econ/.../pdf%26filename3Dpeace.pdf

———— 1931, "Economic Possibilities for Our Grandchildren," in *Essays in Persuasion*, Oxford, UK, Oxford University Press

———— 1936, *The General Theory of Employment, Interest, and Money*, New York, Prometheus Books, (edition 1997)

KHALIL, Elias, 1997, "The Red Queen Paradox: A Proper Name for a Popular Game," *Journal of Institutional Theoretical Economics*, June

KHANNA, Parag, 2008, *The Second World: Empires and Influence in the New Global Order*, London, Allen Lane

KIKER, B.F., 1966, "The Historical Roots of the Concept of Human Capital," *Journal of Political Economy*, October

KISSINGER, Henry, 1961, *The Necessity for Choice: Prospects for American Policy*, New York, Harper

———— 2012, *On China*, New York, Penguin, 2d edition

KLARE, Michael, 2004, *Blood and Oil: The Dangers and Consequences of America's Growing Dependence on Imported Petroleum*, New York, Metropolitan Books

KLEIN, Joel, 2011, "The Failure of American Schools," *The Atlantic*, April 24

———— 2014, *Lessons of Hope: How to Fix Our Schools*, New York, Harper

KNIGHT, Frank, 1921, *Risk, Uncertainty, and Profit*, Boston, Houghton Mifflin

KNORR, Klaus, 1956, *The War Potential of Nations*, Princeton, NJ, Princeton University Press

KOTKIN, Joel, 2010, *The Next Hundred Million: America in 2050*, New York, Penguin Books

KOTKIN, Joel and KISHIMOTO, Yoriko, 1988, *The Third Century: America's Resurgence in the Asian Era*, New York, Crown Publishers

KRUGMAN, Paul, 1997, *The Age of Diminished Expectations: US Economic Policy in the 1990s*, Cambridge, Mass., The MIT Press

KUPCHAN, Charles, 2002, *The End of the American Era*, New York, Alfred A. Knopf (edition 2003, Vintage Books)

KURTH, James, 2009, "Pillars of the Next American Century," *The American Interest*, November 1

KURZWEIL, Ray, 2005, *Singularity Is Near: When Humans Transcend Biology*, New York, Viking Press

———— 2012, *How to Create a Mind: The Secret of Human Thought Revealed*, New York, Viking Press

KWON, Dae-Bong, 2009, "Human Capital and Its Measurement," *OECD World Forum on Statistics, Knowledge, and Policy*, Busan, Korea, October 27–30

LANDES, David, 1966, *The Unbound Prometheus*, Cambridge, UK, Cambridge University Press

LANDES, David, MOKYR, Joel and BAUMOL, William, eds., 2010, *The Invention of Enterprise: Entrepreneurship from Ancient Mesopotamia to Modern Times*, Princeton, NJ, Princeton University Press

LANIER, Jaron, 2013, *Who Owns the Future?* New York, Simon & Schuster

LAQUEUR, Walter, 2007, *The Last Days of Europe: Epitaph for an Old Continent*, New York, Thomas Dunne Books/St. Martin's Press

LAZEAR, Edward, 2002, "Entrepreneurship," *NBER working paper series*, Cambridge, Mass., National Bureau of Economic Research, no. 9109

LEEBAERT, Derek, 2002, *The Fifty Years Wound*, New York, Little Brown

LEONARD, Mark, 2005, *Why Europe Will Run the 21st Century*, New York, HarperCollins

LEVY, Frank and MURNANE, Richard, 2005, *The New Division of Labor: How Computers Are Creating the Next Job Market*, Princeton, NJ, Princeton University Press

LIND, Michael, 2011, "The Case Against 'American Exceptionalism,'" *Salon.com*, June 7

LINDSEY, Brink, 2013, *Human Capitalism: How Economic Growth Has Made Us Smarter—and More Unequal*, Princeton, NJ, Princeton University Press

LIPSET, Seymour Martin, 1996, *American Exceptionalism: A Double-Edged Sword*, New York, W.W. Norton & Company

LIVIO, Mario, 2013, *Brilliant Blunders: From Darwin to Einstein—Colossal Mistakes by Great Scientists That Changed Our Understanding of Life and the Universe*, New York, Simon & Schuster

LOS, Bart, TIMMER, Marcel and de VRIES, Gaaitzen, 2014, "Global Value Chains: 'Factory World' is Emerging," *Vox.org*, May 11

LU, Xiaobo, 2000, *Cadres and Corruption*, Stanford, Calif., Stanford University Press

LUBAR, Steven, 1991, "The Transformation of American Patent Law," *Technology and Culture*, 32(4)

LUCAS, Robert, 1988, "On the Mechanics of Economic Development," *Journal of Monetary Economics*, July

LUCE, Edward, 2012, *Time to Start Thinking: America in the Age of Descent*, New York, Atlantic Monthly Press

LUNDESTAD, Geir, 1990, *The American "Empire" and Other Studies of US Foreign Policy in a Comparative Perspective*, Oxford, UK, Oxford University Press

LUTTWAK, Edward, 1992, "Is America on the Way Down?" *Commentary*, March

———— 2008, "American Declinists: Wrong Again," *American Interest*, 4(2)

MACDONALD, James, 2006, *A Free Nation Deep in Debt: The Financial Roots of Democracy*, Princeton, NJ, Princeton University Press

MACEDO, Stephen, ed., 1997, *Reassessing the Sixties: Debating the Political and Cultural Legacy*, New York, W.W. Norton & Company

MACGREGOR, Richard, 2010, *The Party: The Secret World of China's Communist Rulers*, New York, HarperCollins

MADDISON, Angus, 2007, *Chinese Economic Performance in the Long Run*, Development Centre Studies, Paris, OECD

MAHBUBANI, Kishore, 2008, *The New Asian Hemisphere: The Irresistible Shift of Global Power to the East*, New York, Public Affairs

MANDEL, Michael, 2004, *Rational Exuberance: Silencing the Enemies of Growth*, New York, Harper Collins

MANDELBAUM, Michael, 2002, *The Ideas That Conquered the World: Peace, Democracy, and Free Markets in the Twenty-first Century*, New York, Public Affairs

MANN, Thomas, 2014, "Admit It, Political Scientists; Politics Really Is More Broken than Ever," *The Atlantic*, May 26

MANYIKA, James, BUGHIN, Jacques, LUND, Susan, NOTTEBOHM, Olivia, POULTER, David, JAUCH, Sebastian and RAMASWAMY, Sree, 2014, *Global Flows in a Digital Age: How Trade, Finance, People, and Data Connect the World Economy*, McKinsey Global Institute

MANZI, Jim, 2010, "Keeping America's Edge," *National Affairs*, winter

MARKOVICH, Steven, 2014, "The Income Inequality Debate," *Council on Foreign Relations Backgrounder*, New York, Council on Foreign Relations, February 3

MARSH, Peter, 2012, *The New Industrial Revolution: Consumers, Globalization and the End of Mass Production*, New Haven, Conn., Yale University Press

MASON, David, 2009, *The End of the American Century*, Lanham, Md., Rowman & Littlefield

MATUSOW, Allen, 1984, *The Unraveling of America: A History of Liberalism in the 1960s*, New York, Harper and Row

MAUGERI, Leonardo, 2013, *The Shale Oil Boom: A US Phenomenon*, Geopolitics of Energy Project, Belfer Center for Science and International Affairs, Harvard Kennedy School, June

MAULDIN, John and TEPPER, Jonathan, 2011, *Endgame: The End of the Debt Supercycle and How It Changes Everything*, Hoboken, NJ, John Wiley & Sons

McCLELLAND, David, 1961, *The Achieving Society*, Princeton, NJ, Van Nostrand

McCOY, Terrence, 2012, "How Joseph Stalin Invented 'American Exceptionalism,'" www.theatlantic.com, March 15

McCRAW, Thomas, 2012, *The Founders and Finance: How Hamilton, Gallatin, and Other Immigrants Forged a New Economy*, Cambridge, Mass., The Belknap Press of Harvard University Press

McDOUGALL, Walter, 1985, *The Heavens and the Earth: A Political History of the Space Age*, New York, Basic Books

McKINSEY GLOBAL INSTITUTE, 2013, *Disruptive Technologies: Advances That Will Transform Life, Business, and the Global Economy*, McKinsey & Company

McPHERSON, James, 1988, *Battle Cry of Freedom*, New York, Oxford University Press

MEAD, Walter Russell, 1987, *Mortal Splendor: The American Empire in Transition*, New York, Houghton Mifflin

MELOSI, Martin, 1977, *The Shadow of Pearl Harbor: Political Controversy over the Surprise Attack*, College Station, Texas, Texas A&M University Press

MIGRANYAN, Andranik, 2013, "The Myth of American Exceptionalism," *The National Interest*, October 11

MOHN, Reinhard, 2004, *The Age of New Possibilities*, New York, Crown Publishers

MOKYR, Joel, 1990, *The Lever of Riches: Technological Creativity and Economic Progress*, New York, Oxford University Press

———— 2013, "Is Technological Progress a Thing of the Past?" *Project Syndicate*, September 8

MOORE, Gordon, 1965, "Cramming More Components onto Integrated Circuits," *Electronics*, April 19

MORGAN, Ted, 1999, *A Covert Life. Jay Lovestone: Communist, Anti-Communist, and Spymaster*, New York, Random House

MOROZOV, Evgeny, 2011, *The Net Delusion: The Dark Side of Internet Freedom*, New York, Public Affairs

———— 2013, *To Save Everything, Click Here: The Folly of Technological Solutionism*, New York, Public Affairs

MORRIS, Charles, 2013, *Comeback: America's New Economic Boom*, New York, Public Affairs

MORRIS, Ian, 2010, *Why the West Rules—For Now: The Patterns of History and What They Reveal about the Future*, New York, Profile Books

MORRISON, Wayne, 2013, *China's Economic Rise: History, Trends, Challenges, and Implications for the United States*, Washington, DC, Congressional Research Service, December 17

MURPHY, Kevin; SHLEIFER, Andrei and VISHNY, Robert, 1993, "Why Is Rent-Seeking So Costly to Growth?" *American Economic Review*, 83(2)

MURRAY, Charles, 2013, *American Exceptionalism: An Experiment in History*, Washington, DC, American Enterprise Press

MYRDAL, Gunnar, 1944, *An American Dilemma: The Negro Problem and Modern Democracy*, New York, Harper & Bros

NANAYAKKARA, Rukshana, 2014, "Five Reasons Corruption Is Getting Worse in China," blog.transparency.org, December 3

NATHAN, Andrew and GILLEY, Bruce, 2003, *China's New Rulers*, New York, The New York Review of Books

NAU, Henry, 1990, *The Myth of America's Decline: Leading the World Economy into the 1990s*, New York, Oxford University Press

NELSON LIMERICK, Patricia, 1987, *The Legacy of Conquest: The Unbroken Past of the American West*, New York, Norton

NEUWIRTH, Robert, 2011, *Stealth of Nations: The Global Rise of the Informal Economy*, New York, Pantheon Books

NYE, Joseph, 1990, *Bound to Lead: The Changing Nature of American Power*, New York, Basic Books

———— 2002, *The Paradox of American Power: Why the World's Only Superpower Can't Go It Alone*, New York, Oxford University Press

———— 2010, "The Future of American Power: Dominance and Decline in Perspective," *Foreign Affairs*, 89:6

———— 2014(a), "The Myth of Isolationist America," *Project Syndicate*, February 10

———— 2014(b), "China's Questionable Economic Power," *Project Syndicate*, November 6

OECD, 1998, *Fostering Entrepreneurship*, Paris, Organisation for Economic Co-operation and Development

————, 2011, *An Overview of Growing Income Inequalities in the OECD Countries: Main Findings*, Paris, Organisation for Economic Co-operation and Development

————, 2014, *What Students Know and Can Do: Student Performance in Mathematics, Reading, and Sciences*, Paris, Organisation for Economic Co-operation and Development

OGBURN, William Fielding, 1922, *Social Change with Respect to Culture and Original Nature*, New York, B.W. Huebsch

OLSON, Mancur, 1982, *The Rise and Decline of Nations: Economic Growth Stagflation and Social Rigidities*, New Haven,Conn., Yale University Press

———— 1996, "Distinguished Lecture on Economics in Government. Big Bills Left on the Sidewalk: Why Some Nations Are Rich, and Others Are Poor," *Journal of Economic Perspectives*, spring

ORLOV, Dmitry, 2008, *Reinventing Collapse: The Soviet Example and American Prospects*, Gabriola Island, BC, New Society

O'ROURKE, Kevin and WILLIAMSON, Jeffrey, 2002, "When Did Globalization Begin?" *European Review of Economic History*, 6

O'SULLIVAN, John L., 1839, "The Great Nation of Futurity," *The United States Democratic Review*, 6(23)

——— 1845, "Annexation," *The United States Democratic Review*, July-August

OTTAVIANO, Gianmarco and PERI, Giovanni, 2006, "The Economic Value of Cultural Diversity: Evidence from US Cities," *Journal of Economic Geography*, January, 6(1)

PAINE, Thomas, 1776, *Common Sense*, New York, Penguin (edition 1986)

PALACIOS-HUERTA, Ignacio, ed., 2013, *In 100 Years: Leading Economists Predict the Future*, Cambridge, Mass., The MIT Press

PARFITT, Troy, 2012, *Why China Will Never Rule the World*, Saint John, New Brunswick, Western Hemisphere Press

PARMET, Herbert, 1998, *Eisenhower and the American Crusades*, New York, Transaction Publishers

PAUS, Eva, PRIME, Penelope and WESTERN, Jon, eds., 2009, *Global Giant: Is China Changing the Rules of the Game?* New York, Palgrave

PEI, Minxen, 2007, "Corruption Threatens China's Future," *Policy Brief*, Carnegie Endowment for International Peace, no. 55, October

——— 2010, "China's Not a Superpower," *The Diplomat*, Carnegie Endowment for International Peace, December 29

PEREZ, Carlota, 2002, *Technological Revolutions and Financial Capital: The Dynamics of Bubbles and Golden Ages*, Cheltenham, UK, Edward Elgar

PERROW, Charles, 2002, *Organizing America: Wealth, Power, and the Origins of Corporate Capitalism*, Princeton, NJ, Princeton University Press

PERRY, Mark, 2013, "Thanks to Technology, Americans Spent Dramatically Less on Food than They Did 3 Decades Ago," *AEIdeas*, April 7, www.aei-ideas.org

PETTIS, Michael, 2013, *Avoiding the Fall: China's Economic Restructuring*, Washington, DC, Carnegie Endowment for International Peace

PEW FISCAL ANALYSIS INITIATIVE, 2011, *The Great Debt Shift: Drivers of Debt since 2001*, The Pew Charitable Trusts, April

PEW RESEARCH CENTER, 2014, *Global Attitudes Project*, Washington, DC, PRC

PIGOU, Arthur, 1920, *Economics of Welfare*, London, Macmillan

PIKETTY, Thomas, 2014, *Capital in the Twenty-first Century*, Cambridge, Mass., The Belknap Press of Harvard University

PORTER, Michael, 1990, *The Competitive Advantage of Nations*, New York, The Free Press

PRESTOWITZ, Clyde, 1988, *Trading Places: How We Are Giving Our Future to Japan and How to Reclaim It*, New York, Basic Books

PRITCHETT, Lant and SUMMERS, Larry, 2014, "Asiaphoria Meets Regression to the Mean," *NBER working paper series*, Cambridge, Mass., National Bureau of Economic Research, no. 20573

PRODI, Romano, 2002, *For a New European Entrepreneurship*, speech at the Instituto de Impresa, Madrid, Spain

QUINN, Adam, 2011, "The Art of Declining Politely: Obama's Prudent Presidency and the Waning of American Power," *International Affairs*, 87:4, July

RABINOVICH, Itamar, 2009, "Why American Universities Are the Best—And Why Others Can't Replicate Them," *The American Interest*, May 1

RACHMAN, Gideon, 2011, "American Decline: This Time It's for Real," *Foreign Policy*, no. 184

RATNER, Ely and WRIGHT, Thomas, 2013, "America's Not in Decline—It's on the Rise," *Washington Post*, October 18

RAVITCH, Diane, 2010, *The Death and Life of the Great American School System*, New York, Basic Books

RECTOR, Robert, 2007, "Amnesty Will Cost US Taxpayers at Least $2.6 Trillion," *Heritage Foundation*, June 6

REID, T.R., 2004, *The United States of Europe: The New Superpower and the End of American Supremacy*, New York, Penguin Books

REINHART, Carmen and ROGOFF, Kenneth, 2009, *This Time Is Different: Eight Centuries of Financial Folly*, Princeton, NJ, Princeton University Press

REYNOLDS, David, 2009, *America: Empire of Liberty*, London, Penguin Books

RIDLEY, Matt, 2010, *The Rational Optimist: How Prosperity Evolves*, New York, HarperCollins

RIFKIN, Jeremy, 2004, *The European Dream: How Europe's Vision of the Future Is Quietly Eclipsing the American Dream*, Cambridge, UK, Polity Press

RODRIK, Dani, 1997, *Has Globalization Gone Too Far?* Washington, DC, Institute for International Economics

ROGER, Philippe, 1996, *Rêves et Cauchemars Américains: Les Etats-Unis au Miroir de l'Opinion Publique Française, 1945-1953*, Villeneuve d'Ascq, Presses Universitaires de Septentrion

——— 2002, *L'Ennemi Américain*, Paris, Seuil

ROGERS, Jim, 2013, *Street Smarts: Adventures on the Road and in the Markets*, New York, Crown Publishing

ROLL, Erch, 1930, *An Early Experiment in Industrial Organisation: Being a History of the Firm Boulton & Watt, 1775-1805*, London, Longmans, Green & Co

ROMER, Paul, 1986, "Increasing Returns and Long-Run Growth," *Journal of Political Economy*, 94

——— 1987, "Growth Based on Increasing Returns to Specialization," *American Economic Review*, May

——— 1990, "Endogenous Technological Change," *Journal of Political Economy*, 98

——— 1994, "The Origins of Endogenous Growth Theory," *Journal of Economic Perspectives*, 8

——— 2008, "Economic Growth," *Library of Economics and Liberty* (http://www.econlib.org/library/Enc/EconomicGrowth.html)

ROSEN, Sherwin, 1981, "The Economics of Superstars," *American Economic Review*, 71(5)

ROSENBERG, Nathan, 1982, *Inside the Black Box*, Cambridge, UK, Cambridge University Press

ROUBINI, Nouriel, 2008, *The Decline of the American Empire*, mimeo, August 13

SANANDAJI, Tino, 2010, "The Amazing Truth about PISA Scores: US Beats Europe and Ties with Asia," newgeography.com, December 12 blog post

SANDAGE, Scott, 2005, *Born Losers: The History of Failure in America*, Cambridge, Mass., Harvard University Press

SAY, Jean-Baptiste, 1803, *A Treatise on Political Economy*, Philadelphia, Gregg & Elliott, (edition 1845)

SCHIAVONE, Aldo, 2000, *The End of the Past: Ancient Rome and the Modern West*, Cambridge, Mass., Harvard University Press

SCHILDKRAUT, Deborah, 2014, "Boundaries of American Identity: Evolving Understanding of 'US,'" *Annual Review of Political Science*, vol. 17, January

SCHLESINGER, Arthur, 1959, "Our Ten Contributions to Civilization," *The Atlantic*, March

SCHUCK, Peter and WILSON, James, eds., 2008, *Understanding America: The Anatomy of an Exceptional Nation*, New York, Public Affairs

SCHULTZ, Theodore W., 1961, "Investment in Human Capital," *American Economic Review*, March

——— 1993, *Origins of Increasing Returns*, Oxford, UK, Blackwell

SCHUMPETER, Joseph, 1911, *The Theory of Economic Development*, New Brunswick, NJ, Transaction Publishers

——— 1939, *Business Cycles: A Theoretical, Historical, and Statistical Analysis of the Capitalist Process*, Philadelphia, NJ, Porcupine Press (edition 1982)

————— 1942, *Capitalism, Socialism and Democracy*, New York, Harper and Brothers

SHADBOLT, Nigel and CHUI, Michael, 2014, "Big Data, Big New Businesses," *Project Syndicate*, February 25

SHAMBAUGH, David, 2013, *China Goes Global: The Partial Power*, Oxford, UK, Oxford University Press

SHAWCROSS, William, 2000, *Deliver Us from Evil: Warlords and Peacekeepers in a World of Endless Conflict*, London, Simon & Schuster

SHILLER, Herbert, 1992, *Mass Communications and the American Empire*, Oxford, UK, Westview Press

SHIRK, Susan, 2008, *China: Fragile Superpower*, New York, Oxford University Press

SIDORKIN, Alexander, 2007, "Human Capital and the Labor of Learning: A Case of Mistaken Identity," *Educational Theory*, 57(2)

SIEGFRIED, André, 1955, *America at Mid-century*, New York, Harcourt, Brace & Co

SIMON, Herbert, 1969, *Designing Organizations for an Information-Rich World*, available on http://zeus.zeit.de/2007/39/simon.pdf

SIMON, Julian, 1996, *The Ultimate Resource*, Princeton, NJ, Princeton University Press

SMITH, Adam, 1776, *An Inquiry into the Nature and Causes of the Wealth of Nations*. Reprint edited by Edwin Cannan, Chicago, University of Chicago Press, 1976

SMITH, Rogers, 1997, *Civic Ideals: Conflicting Visions of Citizenship in US History*, New Haven, Conn., Yale University Press

SOLOW, Robert, 1956, "A Contribution to the Theory of Economic Growth," *Quarterly Journal of Economics*, 70

————— 1957, "Technical Change and the Aggregate Production Function," *Review of Economics and Statistics*, 39

SOMBART, Werner, 1906, *Why There Is No Socialism in America*, White Plains, NY, M.E. Sharpe (edition 1976)

SOROS, George, 2014, *The Tragedy of the European Union*, New York, Public Affairs

SPANIER, John, 1959, *The Truman–MacArthur Controversy and the Korean War*, Cambridge, Mass., Harvard University Press

STEAD, W.T., 1902, *The Americanization of the World, or The Trend of the Twentieth Century*, London, Review of Reviews

STEELE GORDON, John, 2004, *An Empire of Wealth: The Epic History of American Economic Power*, New York, HarperCollins

——— 2014, "Entrepreneurship in American History," *Imprimis*, Hillsdale College, 43(2)

STEINFELD, Edward, 2010, *Playing Our Game: Why China's Economic Rise Doesn't Threaten the West*, New York, Oxford University Press

STEVENSON, Howard and JARILLO, Juan Carlos, 1990, "A Paradigm of Entrepreneurship: Entrepreneurial Management," *Strategic Management Journal*, 11

STIGLITZ, Joseph, 2012, *The Price of Inequality: How Today's Divided Society Endangers Our Future*, New York, W.W. Norton & Co

——— 2014, "The Innovation Enigma," *Project Syndicate*, March 9

STRATFOR, 2011(a), *The Geopolitics of United States. Part 1: The Inevitable Empire*, stratfor.com, August 24

STRATFOR, 2011(b), *The Geopolitics of the United States. Part 2: American Identity and the Threats of Tomorrow*, stratfor.com, August 25

SUBRAMANIAN, Arvind, 2011, *Eclipse: Living in the Shadow of China's Economic Dominance*, Washington, DC, Petersen Institute for International Economics

SUOMINEN, Kati, 2012, *Peerless and Periled: The Paradox of American Leadership in the World Economic Order*, Stanford, Calif., Stanford University Press

SWAN, Trevor, 1956, "Economic Growth and Capital Accumulation," *Economic Record*, 32

SYLLA, Richard, 1998, "US Securities Markets and the Banking System, 1790-1840," *Federal Reserve Bank of St. Louis Review*, 80(3)

TAUSSIG, Frank, 1888, *The Tariff History of the United States*, New York, G.P. Putnam & Sons

TELLIS, Ashley, BIALLY, Janice, LAYNE, Christopher and McPHERSON, Melissa, 2000, *Measuring National Power in the Postindustrial Age*, Santa Monica, Calif., RAND Corporation

THE ECONOMIST, 2010, *Data, Data Everywhere*, special report, February 25

——— 2013, *The Gated Globe*, special report, October 12

——— 2014(a), "The Great Expulsion," February 8, p. 18–20

——— 2014(b), *Robots: Immigrants from the Future*, special report, March 29

THE NATIONAL COMMISSION ON FISCAL RESPONSIBILITY AND REFORM, 2010, *The Moment of Truth*, Washington DC

THUROW, Lester, 1992, *Head to Head. The Coming Battle among Japan, Europe, and America*, New York, Morrow

——— 2002, *Fortune Favors the Bold*, Cambridge, Mass., The MIT Press

TIEZZI, Shannon, 2013, "China's Looming Social Security Crisis," *The Diplomat*, November 22

TODD, Emmanuel, 2002, *Après l'Empire: Essai sur la Décomposition du Système Americain*, Paris, Ed. Gallimard

TRACHTENBERG, Mark, 2014, *Assessing Soviet Economic Performance during the Cold War: A Failure of Intelligence?* mimeo, Department of Political Science, University of California, Los Angeles

TRACY, James, ed., 1990, *The Rise of Merchant Empires*, Cambridge, UK, Cambridge University Press

TULLOCK, Gordon, 1967, "The Welfare Costs of Tariffs, Monopolies, and Theft," *Western Economic Journal*, 5(3)

TURNER, Adair, 2014, "The High-Tech, High-Touch Economy," *Project Syndicate*, April 16

TURNER, Frederick Jackson, 1893, "The Significance of the Frontier in American History, available at www.learner.org/workshops/.../docs/turner.html

——— 1921, *The Frontier in American History*, New York, Henry Holt and Company

TURNER, Michael, 2014, "Inequality Myths," *National Review (Online)*, May 14

VAN OVERTVELDT, Johan, 2007, *The Chicago School: How the University of Chicago Assembled the Thinkers Who Revolutionized Economics and Business*, Chicago, Agate Publishing

——— 2011, *The End of the Euro: The Uneasy Future of the European Union*, Chicago, Agate Publishing

VAUGHN, Karen, 1994, *Austrian Economics in America: The Migration of a Tradition*, New York, W.W. Norton & Company

VIJG, Jan, 2011, *The American Technological Challenge: Stagnation and Decline in the 21st Century*, New York, Algora Publishing

VOGEL, Ezra, 1979, *Japan as Number One: Lessons for America*, Cambridge, Mass., Harvard University Press

——— 2011, *Deng Xiaoping and the Transformation of China*, Cambridge, Mass., Harvard University Press

WADHWA, Vivek, 2012, *The Immigration Exodus: Why America Is Losing the Global Race to Capture Entrepreneurial Talent*, Philadelphia, Wharton Digital Press

WADHWA, Vivek, SAXENIAN, AnnaLee, RISSING, Ben and GEREFFI, Gary, 2007, *America's New Immigrant Entrepreneurs*, Kansas City, MO, The Kaufman Foundation

WALT, Stephen, 2011, "The Myth of American Exceptionalism," *Foreign Policy*, November

WALTER, Carl and HOWIE, Fraser, 2011, *Red Capitalism: The Fragile Foundation of China's Extraordinary Rise*, Hoboken, NJ, John Wiley and Sons

WEBER, Max, 1930, *The Protestant Ethic and the Spirit of Capitalism*, London, Allen and Unwin

WEINBERG, Albert, 1935, *Manifest Destiny*, Baltimore, The John Hopkins University Press

WEITZMAN, Martin, 1998, "Recombinant Growth," *Quarterly Journal of Economics*, 113(2)

WESTAD, Odd Arne, 2005, *The Global Cold War: Third World Interventions and the Making of Our Times*, Cambridge, UK, Cambridge University Press

WHITE, William, 2014, "The Prudential Regulation of Financial Institutions: Why Regulatory Responses to the Crisis Might Not Prove Efficient," *OECD Economics Department Working Paper*, Paris, OECD, no. 1108

WHYTE, William, 1960, *The Organization Man*, London, Penguin

WILSON, Dominic and PURUSHOTHAMAM, Roopa, 2003, "Dreaming with BRICs: The Path to 2050," *Global Economics Paper*, Goldman Sachs, no. 99, October

WOHLFORTH, William, 1999, "The Stability of a Unipolar World," *International Security*, 24(1)

WOOD, Gordon, 2011, *The Idea of America: Reflections on the Birth of the United States*, New York, Penguin

WORLD BANK, 2006, *Where Is the Wealth of Nations? Measuring Capital for the 21st Century*, Washington, DC, World Bank Publications

————— 2012, *Information and Communications for Development 2012: Maximizing Mobile*, Washington, DC, World Bank Publications

WU, Harry, 2006, *The Chinese GDP Growth Rate Puzzle: How Fast Has the Chinese Economy Grown?* paper prepared for the 29th General Conference of the International Association for Research in Income and Wealth, Joensuu, Finland, August 20–26

XUECUN, Murong, 2012, "No Roads Are Straight Here," *The New York Times*, May 8

YERGIN, Daniel, 2014, "The Global Impact of US Shale," *Project Syndicate*, January 8

ZAKARIA, Fareed, 2008, *The Post-American World*, New York, W.W. Norton & Company

ZHU, Xiadong, 2013, "Understanding China's Growth: Past, Present, and Future," *Journal of Economic Perspectives*, 26(4)

ZOELLICK, Robert, 2000, "Campaign 2000: A Republican Foreign Policy," *Foreign Affairs*, January/February

ZUCKERMAN, Gregory, 2013, *The Frackers: The Outrageous Inside Story of the New Billionaire Wildcatters*, New York, Portfolio/Penguin

Endnotes

1   Dowd, 2007, p. 1.
2   Blog post by McCoy of December 5, 2010 on www.tomdispatch.com
    /archive/175327/.
3   Title of a major piece Beinart wrote in *The National Journal*, February 3, 2014.
4   www.zerohedge.com/news/2014-03-11/55.
5   *Ibid.*
6   Stratfor, 2011(a), p. 15.
7   Rogers, 2013, p. 16.
8   Luce as quoted in Bell, 1975, p. 203.
9   Stratfor, 2011(a), p. 15.
10 This is a reference to Francis Fukuyama's 1989 article and subsequent 1992 book
    that both contained a much subtler argumentation on liberal democracy's future. See
    Fukuyama, 1989 and 1992.
11 Speech of President George H.W. Bush to Congress, March 6, 1991.
12 See, for example, Ferguson, 2010 and Luce, 2012.
13 David Malpass in *The American Spectator*, May 2011.
14 For a very interesting comparison between the Roman Empire and the United States,
    see Cullen, 2007.
15 W. James Antle III in *The American Spectator*, May 2011.
16 Manzi, 2010.
17 Dyer, 2014.
18 Yew as quoted on the *Forbes* website on February 13, 2013.
19 Tsvi Bisk in a blog post on May, 4, 2012 on www.wfs.org/blogs.
20 McGurn in *The American Spectator*, May 2011.
21 Joffe, 2014.
22 Dyer, 2014, p. 9.
23 Dowd, 2007, p. 1.

24   Larry Summers in a speech before the Economic Policy Institute, Washington, DC,
      December 13, 2010, as reprinted in Subramanian, 2011, p. 3, 4.
25   Joffe, 2014, p. 279 (fn. 83).
26   Ceaser, 2003.
27   Kant as quoted in Gerbi, 1973, p. 330, 331.
28   Moore, Thomas, "To Thomas Hume Esq, M.D.," http://sailor.gutenberg.org/
      etexto5/7cptm10.txt.
29   Darwin, 1845.
30   The Linguet story as recounted in Roger, 1996.
31   Dickens as quoted in Nye, 2010, p. 3.
32   The most authoritative book on the history of the Civil War is still McPherson, 1988.
33   Madison as quoted in *Time*, April 7, 2011.
34   The North's population was four times that of the South, while the industrial and
      economic base of the North was ten times that of the South. See Stratfor, 2011(b).
35   Dowd, 2007, p. 2.
36   Reynolds, 2009, p. 577.
37   McCraw, 2012, p. 2.
38   Reynolds, 2009, p. 217.
39   Chevalier, 1866.
40   Bryce, 1888, vol. 2, p. 235–236.
41   Joffe, 2014, p. 61.
42   See Perrow, 2002.
43   For more on this and the subsequent turbulence, see, for example, Glasner and
      Cooley, 1997 and Foner, 2002. For a monetarist view on 1873, see Friedman, 1989.
44   Freud as quoted in Jones, 1961, p. 270.
45   Stead, 1902, preface.
46   Bell, 1975, p. 200.
47   Stead, 1902, preface.
48   Roosevelt as quoted in Cumings, 2009, p. 138.
49   Hodgson, 2009, p. 68.
50   Stalin as quoted in Reynolds, 2009, p. 337.
51   Hoover as quoted in Reynolds, 2009, p. 335.
52   With respect to the mistakes in banking and monetary affairs, the standard reference
      remains Friedman and Schwartz, 1963.
53   Edmund Wilson in Alexander, 1969, p. 2.
54   Hitler as quoted in Dowd, 2007, p. 2.
55   Hitler as quoted in Compton, 1968, p. 17.
56   Melosi, 1977, p. xi.
57   Manzi, 2010.
58   Truman as quoted in Schiller, 1992, p. 50.
59   Laski as quoted in Lundestad, 1990, p. 39.
60   Reynolds, 2009, p. 384.
61   See, for example, Leebaert, 2002.
62   Stalin as quoted in Gaddis, 1997, p. 109.
63   This conflict sharply divided the nation for months. See Spanier, 1959.
64   MacArthur as quoted in Kagan, 2012, p. 111.
65   Reynolds, 2009, p. 393.

66 Brogan, 1953.
67 Hardly any attention was paid to the fact that Sputnik stopped transmitting after three weeks and literally fell out of the sky a few weeks later.
68 McDougall, 1985, p. 154.
69 Rayburn as quoted in Parmet, 1998, p. 537.
70 Khrushchev as quoted in Reynolds, 2009, p. 403.
71 Mao as quoted in Westad, 2005, p. 184.
72 See Westad, 2005.
73 Kissinger, 1961, p. 3.
74 *Newsweek* as quoted in Reynolds, 2009, p. 447.
75 Still the best account and analysis of this breathtaking period in world history is Fursenko and Naftali, 1997.
76 Kennedy as quoted in Reynolds, 2009, p. 443.
77 Mansfield in Macedo, ed., 1997, p. 21
78 Carson, 1962.
79 Harrington, 1963.
80 Matusow, 1984.
81 Kissinger as quoted in Dowd, 2007, p. 3.
82 Reynolds, 2009, p. 480.
83 Bell, 1975, p. 204, 197.
84 Hodgson, 2009, p. 110.
85 Brandon, 1974, p. 3.
86 Reynolds, 2009, p. 475.
87 As quoted in Westad, 2005, p. 241.
88 Carter as quoted by Matt Latimer in *The American Spectator*, May 2011.
89 "Address to the Nation on Energy and National Goals: The 'Malaise Speech,'" July 15, 1979, available at www.presidency.ucsb.edu.
90 Rajaratnam in the *Wall Street Journal*, June 22, 1979.
91 Lord as quoted in *Newsweek*, November 26, 1979.
92 Huntington, 1988, p. 95.
93 Reynolds, 2009, p. 507.
94 Ferguson, 2004, p. 262. Caspar Weinberger was Ronald Reagan's hawkish secretary of defense.
95 Reagan as quoted in Reynolds, 2009, p. 514.
96 Vogel, 1979.
97 Crichton, 1992, p. 349. On the superiority of the Japanese model, see also Fallows, 1989.
98 The boom lasted until 2007, the year the financial crisis started to gain traction.
99 Morita and Ishihara as quoted in Flora Lewis, "Japan's Looking Glass," *New York Times*, November 8, 1989.
100 Prestowitz as quoted in *Time*, July 4, 1988.
101 Prestowitz, 1988, p. 493.
102 Senator Paul Tsongas as quoted in the *New York Times*, February 17, 1992.
103 Kennedy, 1987. For powerful counters to Kennedy's arguments, see Huntington, 1988; Nau, 1990; and Nye, 1990.
104 Kennedy, 1987, p. 55.
105 Kotkin and Kishimoto, 1988.

106 Schmidt as quoted in Joffe, 2014, p. 31.

107 As told in Acemoglu and Robinson, 2012, p. 128.

108 Jim Rogers, colorful as ever, describes it as follows: "The Soviets did not have anything because nobody produced anything, and nobody produced anything because prices were set so low. When I was driving through Russia on my motorcycle trip, kids were using loaves of bread for footballs. The price of bread was set at an artificially low level, and it was cheaper to buy a succession of loaves than it was to buy a football (if you could find one to buy)." Rogers, 2013, p. 207.

109 Another element of the USSR's downfall was its relative lack of sophistication in the worlds of computers, electronics, and information processing. For more on this, see, for example, Dawisha, 1990.

110 Kennedy, 2002(a). Shortly afterward, he concluded that the overwhelming military dominance of the United States was mainly due to spectacular and unforeseeable developments in military technology. See Kennedy, 2002(b).

111 Krauthammer in the *Washington Post*, March 22, 1991.

112 One of the most stunning examples ever of French cynicism toward the United States was expressed by sociologist and philosopher Jean Baudrillard, who shortly after the attacks of 9/11 wrote: "how all the world without exception dreamt of this event, for no one can avoid dreaming of the destruction of a power that has become hegemonic. … It is they who acted, but we who wanted the deed" (Baudrillard as quoted in Ajami, 2003). In 1925, French Communist writer Louis Aragon expressed the following wish: "Let faraway America and its white buildings come crashing down." (Aragon as quoted in Roger, 2002, p. 439.) A few decades later, another French writer, Henry de Montherlant, tried to outdo Aragon: "One nation that manages to lower intelligence, morality, human quality on nearly all the surface of the earth, such a thing has never been seen before in the existence of the planet. I accuse the United States of being in a permanent state of crime against humankind" (de Montherlant, 1963, p. 265).

113 Chirac as quoted in Shawcross, 2000, p. 211. Compared to these words, the claim of the 19th century French poet Charles Baudelaire that America is a "great hunk of barbarism illuminated by gas" sounds rather inoffensive (Baudelaire as quoted in Ceaser, 1997, p. 11).

114 Zoellick, 2000.

115 Ikenberry, 2002, p. 1.

116 Esler, 1998, p. 7.

117 See, for example, Huntington, 1999 and Nye, 2002.

118 Luttwak, 1992. Fifteen years later, the same author declared, "the declinists, wrong again."

119 Calleo, 1992.

120 Thurow, 1992.

121 Pinter as quoted in Conrad, 2014, p. 322.

122 Pinter as quoted in the *New York Times*, December 8, 2005.

123 Todd, 2002.

124 Kupchan, 2002.

125 Reid, 2004.

126 Rifkin, 2004.

127 Zakaria, 2008. Only four years earlier, Zakaria had argued on BBC News that unipolar dominance of the United States was unlike anything seen since Rome. Zakaria on BBC News, January 26, 2004.

128 Bacevich, 2008.
129 See, for example, Khanna, 2008; Mason, 2009; Ferguson, 2010; Quinn, 2011 and Luce, 2012.
130 John Gray in *The Guardian*, September 28, 2008.
131 *New York Times*, April 4, 2009.
132 See, for example, Mahbubani, 2008.
133 Orlov, 2008, p. 104.
134 Roubini, 2008, p. 3.
135 Ferguson in the *Washington Post*, September 21, 2008.
136 Flynn, 2008, p. 1, 8.
137 *Der Spiegel*, 2010.
138 Suominen, 2012, p. xi.
139 Rogers, 2013, p. 166.
140 Rachman, 2011.
141 Hill, 2010.
142 Gross, 2012.
143 *The Economist*, July 14, 2012, p. 8.
144 Emmott, 2008.
145 Emmott, 2012.
146 Ratner and Wright, 2013.
147 *The Economist*, February 1, 2014, p. 7.
148 See, for example, Zakaria, 2008 and Haass, 2013.
149 See Berkowitz, 2007 for more on this qualification.
150 With respect to this last element, see also, for example, Black, 2008.
151 Mandelbaum, 2002.
152 Joffe, 2014. See also discussion in Chapter 3 of this book.
153 Rogers, 2013, p. 29.
154 See, for example, Kurzweil, 2005 and 2012.
155 Chorost, 2011.
156 http://forumblog.org/2014/02/top-ten-emerging-technologies-2014/.
157 *Ibid.*
158 *Ibid.*
159 *Ibid.*
160 McKinsey, 2013.
161 Late in April 2014, reports emerged that an Israeli company had developed a technology that allows recharge of batteries of cell phones, iPads, and other electronics in less than 30 seconds. This device, it was claimed, was derived from research on Alzheimer's disease. Interesting that such a different subject area would yield such results.
162 Heck et al., 2014.
163 LASER stands for light amplification by stimulated emission of radiation.
164 Charles H. Townes, "The First Laser," in Garwin and Lincoln, 2003.
165 As quoted in Campbell-Kelly and Aspray, 1996, p. 147.
166 *The Economist*, 2014 (b), p. 9.
167 See *Popular Science*, June 4, 2004.
168 Levy and Murnane, 2005.
169 Mandel, 2004, p. xi–xii.
170 Krugman, 1997, p. 11.

171 Cowen, 2011; Gordon, 2012; Vijg, 2011; Huesemann and Huesemann, 2011; Heidegger, 1953; Ellul, 1964; and Kasparov, Levchin, and Thiel, 2012. There are also truly eccentric figures like Theodore Kaczynski, also known as the Unabomber.

172 Stiglitz, 2014.

173 Matt Ridley correctly notes that "arch-pessimists are feted, showered with honors and rarely challenged, let alone confronted with their past mistakes." Ridley, 2010, p. 295.

174 Gordon, 2012, p. 1.

175 Cowen, 2011, p. 6, 7.

176 Deaton in Palacios-Huerta, 2013, p. 38.

177 Ridley, 2010; Mokyr, 2013; Baily, Manyika, and Gupta, 2013; Brynjolfsson and McAfee, 2014; Weitzman, 1998; Romer, 2008; and Simon, 1996.

178 Keynes, 1931.

179 See, for example, on such issues Ignatieff, 2014 and Brynjolfsson and McAfee, 2014.

180 For an excellent survey of the issues involved in this problem of inequality, see Markovich, 2014. In his book *Capital*, French economist Thomas Piketty argued that rising inequality remains a basic law of capitalist development (Piketty, 2014). Acemoglu and Robinson, 2014 is one of the most powerful rebuttals of Piketty's argument.

181 Morozov, 2011; See also Morozov, 2013 and Lanier, 2013.

182 Chorost, 2011, p. 7, 10.

183 Romer, 2008.

184 Ridley, 2010, p. 358–359.

185 Brynjolfsson and McAfee, 2014, p. 9.

186 Acemoglu in Palacios-Huerta, 2013, p. 25.

187 Glaeser in Palacios-Huerta, 2013, p. 60.

188 Mokyr, 2013.

189 See, for example, *The Economist*, 2010 and also Shadbolt and Chui, 2014. For a critical view on Big Data, see Harford, 2014.

190 Mohn, 2004, p. 17.

191 Morris, 2010, p. 27.

192 Arthur, 2009.

193 Romer, 2008.

194 Ogburn, 1922.

195 Moore, 1965.

196 See Adam Sneed's overview on Slate.com, May 3, 2012.

197 Baumol, Litan, and Schramm, 2007, p. 90

198 Livio, 2013.

199 Immelt in the *Washington Post*, December 10, 2009.

200 For more on the history of the Luddites and their modern-day counterparts, see Jones, 2006.

201 On the history of human capital, see Kiker, 1966.

202 Arrow, 1962(a), 1962(b).

203 Keesing, 1966.

204 The importance of human capital is best summarized in Becker, 1993. See on these issues also Van Overtveldt, 2007, especially Chapter 4.

205 For the origins of these and other definitions of human capital, see Kwon, 2009 and the references in that paper.

206 *Ibid.*

207 It includes, for example, organizational, social, and interpersonal skills that also contribute to welfare and well-being.

208 Jorgenson and Fraumeni, 1989.

209 Solow, 1956 and 1957. After Solow, Trevor Swan contributed in important ways to the neoclassical growth model. See Swan, 1956.

210 On the basis of research done by British economist Roy Harrod and his American colleague Evsy Domar. Harrod and Domar worked independently of each other.

211 Schumpeter, 1939, p. 86.

212 Abramovitz, 1952. This paper is also the source of the other quotes in this paragraph.

213 See, especially, Landes, 1966; Rosenberg, 1982; and Mokyr, 1990.

214 Schumpeter, 1942, p. 106.

215 Chandler, 1977 and 1990 on the dominance and desirability of large entities, and Whyte, 1960 on the archetypical organization man most able to run efficiently these behemoths.

216 Chandler, 1977.

217 Abramovitz, 1952.

218 Schultz, 1961, p. 6.

219 Schultz as quoted in Van Overtveldt, 2007, p. 112.

220 Arrow, 1962(a).

221 Pigou, 1920.

222 Ronald Coase showed that in a hypothetical world with no transaction costs, private parties would negotiate a way out of the externality problem. See Coase, 1960.

223 Lucas, 1988.

224 Romer, 1986 and 1990.

225 Jones, 2005.

226 Weitzman, 1998, p. 357.

227 Jacobs, 1969.

228 Glaeser, 2011, p. 1, 7, 8.

229 Porter, 1990.

230 For more on this, see the discussion in Van Overtveldt, 2007, Chapter 4. See also Ehrlich, 2007.

231 Research into agricultural advancements was the genesis of this. A seminal research paper in this respect was Griliches, 1957.

232 See several contributions in Becker, 1993, but especially Chapter 7. See also, for example, Lucas, 1988; Acemoglu, 1996; and Hansen and Knowles, 1998. Schultz, 1993 also deals extensively with increasing returns to scale.

233 See, for example, Becker, 1993 and Sidorkin, 2007.

234 Cohen, 2012, p. xix.

235 Lindsey, 2013.

236 Romer, 1987, p. 56.

237 Annunziata et al., 2014, p. 11.

238 Baumol, Litan, and Schramm, 2007, p. 9.

239 Schiavone as quoted in Cohen, 2012, p. 9.

240 Rent seeking was first elaborately analyzed in Tullock, 1967. For an in-depth discussion of the consequences of rent seeking for economic growth, see Murphy, Shleifer, and Vishny, 1993.

241 On these institutional issues, see Acemoglu and Robinson, 2012.

242 Baumol, Litan, and Schramm, 2007, p. 90.

243 For an insightful story on the intense competition between technology companies like Google, Apple, Facebook, and Amazon, see *The Economist*, 2012, "Another Game of Thrones," December 1, p. 25–28.

244 William Baumol in Landes, Mokyr, and Baumol, 2010, p. ix.

245 Lazear, 2002, p. 1.

246 Porter, 1990.

247 Prodi, 2002, p. 1.

248 *The Economist*, July 20, 2013, p. 56.

249 For more on the "Austrian school," see, for example, Vaughn, 1994.

250 See, for example, Schumpeter, 1911 and 1939.

251 Interview with Gary Becker, January 4, 2007.

252 OECD, 1998, p. 11.

253 Drucker, 1985, p. 30.

254 For an early approach like this one, see McClelland, 1961. See also, for example, Stevenson and Jarillo, 1990.

255 Weber, 1930.

256 Kets de Vries, 1977.

257 Keynes, 1936, p. 162. Modern-day aspects of animal spirits are further analyzed in Akerlof and Shiller, 2009.

258 See Acemoglu and Robinson, 2012 for more on the characteristics of an appropriate institutional environment for productive entrepreneurship.

259 On these issues, see Granovetter, 1985.

260 This is not to say that no communist regime has entrepreneurship. In those situations, entrepreneurship largely takes the form of bureaucratic infighting, which seldom benefits a society as a whole but often benefits those who successfully navigate it.

261 Gilpin, 1975, p. 70.

262 Christensen, 1997.

263 Baumol, 2002(b), p. 7.

264 Heck et al., 2014.

265 Galbraith, 1956, p. 86.

266 Baumol, Litan, and Schramm, 2007, p. 86, 87.

267 See, especially, Chapter 3 in Audretsch, Keilbach, and Lehman, 2006.

268 Audretsch, Keilbach, and Lehman, 2006, p. 35.

269 Annunziata et al., 2014, p. 11.

270 Reference can be made here to the work of French authors Richard Cantillon (1680–1734), Nicolas Baudeau (1730–1792), and Jean-Baptiste Say (1767–1832). Frank Knight (1885–1972), one of the founding fathers of the Chicago School of economics, also stressed the link between uncertainty and entrepreneurship. See Cantillon, 1755; Baudeau, 1767; Say, 1803; and Knight, 1921.

271 Isenberg, 2013.

272 Audretsch, Keilbach, and Lehman, 2006, p. 19.

273 Olson, 1996.

274 Baumol and Strom in Landes, Mokyr, and Baumol, 2010, p. 531.

275 The full story of the remarkable partnership is still best told in Roll, 1930.

276 David Landes in Landes, Mokyr, and Baumol, 2010, p. 5.

277 Held et al., 1999, p. 2.

278 James, 2009, p. 5.
279 Frank and Gills, 1993; Frank, 1998 and Bentley, 1993.
280 Bentley, 1999, p. 7
281 Findlay and O'Rourke, 2008.
282 Frank and Gills, 1993, p. 3.
283 Friedman distinguishes three episodes of globalization: the globalization of countries (1492–1800), the globalization of companies (1800–2000), and the globalization of individuals (2000–). See Friedman, 2005.
284 O'Rourke and Williamson, 2002, p. 47.
285 Keynes, 1919, p. 6.
286 All the data in the next paragraphs are taken from *The Economist*, 2013 and from Manyika et al., 2014.
287 Manyika et al., 2014.
288 Data on cellular phone subscriptions are from the World Bank, 2012.
289 *The Economist*, 2013, p. 1.
290 Los, Timmer, and de Vries, 2014, p. 4.
291 Dachs, Stehrer, and Zahradnik, 2014.
292 *Financial Times*, December 8, 2013.
293 *Ibid*, p. 14.
294 Manyika et al., 2014, p. 1.
295 Smith, 1776, p. 21.
296 Manyika et al., 2014, p. 2.
297 For an excellent description of how intensely and surprisingly this entrepreneurial economy has developed worldwide, and even in the least developed countries, see Neuwarth, 2011.
298 Manyika et al., 2014, p. 3.
299 Baumol, 2002(a), p. viii (italics in the original).
300 Bordo, 2002, p. 21.
301 James, 2009, p. 7.
302 James, 2009, p. 22.
303 Turner, 2014.
304 *Ibid*.
305 *Ibid*.
306 This argument, as well as that of the third process discussed below, was inspired by Haldane, 2013.
307 Haldane, 2013, p. 3. This paper contains many interesting references to the research on the phenomena under discussion.
308 White, 2014, p. 6. See also Ball, 2012 on issues of societal complexity.
309 White, 2014, p. 6.
310 Simon, 1969, as quoted in Haldane, 2013, p. 5.
311 Haldane, 2013, p. 5.
312 Brynjolfsson and McAfee, 2014, p. 90.
313 Gross, 2012, p. 18.
314 Easterbrook, 2009, p. xii, xvi.
315 Brynjolfsson and McAfee, 2014, p. 11.
316 See, for example, Acemoglu and Autor, 2010.
317 Frank and Cook, 1996.

318 Gilpin, 1981.

319 Title of a piece published by Subramanian in *Foreign Affairs*, Sept/Oct 2011.

320 See, for example, the reporting in the *New York Times* of April 29, 1958 ("Allen Dulles Sees US Peril in Soviet's Economic Rise") and of November 14, 1959 ("Soviet Closing Output Gap, Allen Dulles Warns US."

321 See the analysis and the many references in Trachtenberg, 2014.

322 Wilson and Purushothamam, 2003. BRIC stands for a group of four important emerging economies: China, India, Brazil, and Russia. The acronym is not terribly useful, not least of which because China's overall GDP is 1.5 times larger than the three other countries *combined*.

323 See, for example, Jacques, 2009; Anderson, 2009; and Subramanian, 2011. For a powerful counter-argumentation, see, for example, Shirk, 2008; Steinfeld, 2010; Beckley, 2011; Walter and Howie, 2011; Joffe, 2014; and Fenby, 2014.

324 Amsden, 2001.

325 GDP is the total value of goods and services produced within an economy. Most of the time GDP is measured in terms of annual production.

326 A more complete indicator of individual human well-being is the human development index of the United Nations. GDP per capita is one of the parameters that make up the human development index.

327 For more on this, specifically with respect to China, see, for example, Cooper, 2005.

328 Taking into account the huge overcapacities that have been built up in the industrial and real estate sectors of the Chinese economy, the gap with the US, where also overcapacities exist but to a much smaller degree, would increase substantially. For more about overcapacity in China, see the section "Zombification" later in this chapter.

329 China annually adds $644 billion to its GDP, the US $504 billion. The difference is $140 billion. Given the gap between American and Chinese GDP in 2013 of $7.6 trillion ($16.8 – $9.2) it takes 54 years to bridge that gap (7,600 divided by 140).

330 Beckley, 2011, p. 44. On "rising" and "catching up," see also Chestnut, Sheena, and Johnston, Alistair, "Is China Rising?" in Paus, Prime, and Western, 2009.

331 Pritchett and Summers, 2014.

332 IMF data reveal that many developing countries often experience bursts of high growth. In 2013, for example, six countries saw their economies grow by more than 10%: South Soudan (27.1%), Sierra Leone (20.1%), Paraguay (13.6%), Mongolia (11.7%), Kyrgyz Republic (10.5%) and Turkmenistan (10.2%). Only Mongolia and Turkmenistan sustained high-level growth for more than a few years.

333 Gerschenkron, 1962.

334 Joffe, 2014, p. 83.

335 Joffe as quoted on thedailybeast.com, November 17, 2013.

336 In this case, China catches up to the tune of $32 billion per year (368 minus 336). To bridge a gap of $7.6 trillion, one needs 238 years (7,600 divided by 32).

337 Increasing both GDP per capita numbers for 2013 by 30,000 leads to $83,001 for the US and $41,868 for China; 83,001 divided by 41,868 equals 1.97.

338 World Bank, 2006.

339 Easterbrook, 2009, p. xiii.

340 Nye, 2010, p. 7–8.

341 Reference is made here to the Programme for International Students Assessment (PISA) investigations of the OECD. See OECD, 2014.

342 Sanandaji, 2010.

343 Halper in *The American Spectator*, May 2011.

344 Capelli, 2014.

345 Shanker as quoted in Klein, 2011.

346 Chetty, Friedman, and Rockoff, 2011.

347 Klein, 2011. See also Klein, 2014.

348 Kurth, 2009.

349 See, for example, Abdulkadiroglu et al., 2009.

350 The only three non-American institutions in the top 20 are two British institutions (Oxford at 9 and University College London at 20) and one Swiss (Federal Institute of Technology, Zurich at 19).

351 For a short historical overview on research universities, see Atkinson and Blanpied, 2008.

352 Atkinson and Blanpied, 2008, p. 46.

353 Atkinson and Blanpied, 2008, p. 30.

354 All the quotes in the above paragraph are from Rabinovich, 2009.

355 Just to avoid any misunderstanding: the above arguments are analytical conclusions, not value judgments.

356 See, for example, Glaeser, Ponzetto, and Shleifer, 2007.

357 Cain in Landes, Mokyr, and Baumol, 2010, p. 331.

358 I am referring to a single person known as king of England and Ireland as James I and king of Scotland as James VI.

359 These settlements were not the very first permanent European settlements in what would become the United States. In 1565 Spain established permanent settlements in Florida in 1565 and in what eventually became parts of Texas and New Mexico in 1598.

360 Steele Gordon, 2014, p. 3.

361 *The Economist*, March 12, 2009; this is also the source of the next quote in this paragraph.

362 Mokyr, 1990, p. 302.

363 Steele Gordon, 2014, p. 4

364 *Ibid.*

365 Acemoglu and Robinson, 2012.

366 Lamoreaux in Landes, Mokyr, and Baumol, 2010, p. 369.

367 Lubar, 1991, p. 934.

368 Specifically, in the section "Self-Interest Well Understood."

369 Sylla, 1998, p. 456.

370 Perze, 2002.

371 Steele Gordon, 2014, p. 4. That failure was and is more acceptable in the United States than in most other places does not mean that it is without consequences at the personal level. See Sandage, 2005.

372 Gros, 2014, p. 2.

373 I return to the importance of immigration for the successes of the United States later in this chapter. See the section "Makers, Not Takers."

374 See, for example, Ottaviano and Peri, 2006.

375 Nye, 2010, p. 7.

376 See, for example, the reporting in the *Financial Times*, September 14, 2014.

377 On isolationism and foreign policy, see Crabb, 1986.

378 Eckes, 1995.

379 As quoted on the Huffington Post website, September 12, 2010.

380 Henry Clay as quoted in Lind, 2011.

381 Taussig, 1888.

382 For more historical context on this exorbitant privilege, see Eichengreen, 2011.

383 Buchanan, 1998, p. 224.

384 Fletcher, 2010.

385 Fletcher on the Huffington Post website on September 12, 2010: "America Was Founded as a Protectionist Nation."

386 Pew Research Center, 2014.

387 Ewing, 2012, p. 4.

388 Bhidé, 2008.

389 Easterbrook, 2009, p. 208.

390 Berchem as quoted in the *Financial Times*, September 14, 2014.

391 Hirschman, 1958. Next to the polarization effect Hirschman also referred to the "diffusive effect," the tendency of growth to trickle down to more peripheral areas.

392 Siegfried, 1955, p. 6, 7.

393 de Tocqueville, Alexis, 1865, *Oeuvres Complètes*, vol. VIII, Paris, M; Lévy Frères, p. 253.

394 Dowd, 2007, p. 7.

395 Brynjolfsson and McAfee, 2014, p. 178.

396 Deaton in Palacios-Huerta, 2013, p. 38.

397 Olson, 1982.

398 Lee Kuan Yew as quoted on the website of *Forbes* magazine on February 13, 2013.

399 *Ibid.*

400 Summers in a speech at the Economic Policy Institute in Washington DC, December 1, 2010 as reprinted in Subramanian, 2011, p. 4.

401 Manzi, 2010.

402 Hodgson, 2009, p. xii.

403 Roosevelt as quoted in Reynolds, 2009, p. 346.

404 Kupchan as quoted on December 2, 2002 on Salon.com.

405 Gross, 2012, p. 23.

406 Wohlforth, 1999, p. 17.

407 Halper in *The American Spectator*, May 2011.

408 Clive Crook on the Bloomberg website, February 9, 2014.

409 *Ibid.*

410 The quintessential statement of American exceptionalism is Lipset, 1996. For an extremely politicized version of American exceptionalism, see Gingrich, 2011. For powerful statements against the idea of American exceptionalism, see, for example, Hodgson, 2009; Lind, 2011; Walt, 2011 and Migranyan, 2013. See also Breinart, 2014.

411 Ceaser, 2012, p. 1.

412 Schildkraut, 2014, p. 442.

413 Bell, 1975, p. 199. For more on manifest destiny in general, see Weinberg, 1935.

414 Johanssen in Haynes and Morris, 1997, p. 18. See also Paine, 1776.

415 O'Sullivan, 1845.

416 O'Sullivan, 1839.

417 Hector St. John de Crèvecoeur as quoted on MyAmerica.be by Michael Jay Friedman in the posting "American Identity: Ideas, Not Ethnicity" (Friedman, 2007).

418 De Tocqueville produced *Democracy in America* in two volumes, the first published in 1835, the second in 1840.

419 De Tocqueville, 1835–40, p. 430.

420 Beveridge as quoted in Ceaser, 2012, p. 9.

421 Wuthnow in Schuck and Wilson, 2008, p. 289 and 265.

422 Kossuth as quoted in Wood, 2011, p. 321.

423 http://showcase.netins.net/web/creative/lincoln/speeches/congress.htm.

424 Winthrop as quoted in Ceaser, 2012, p. 5.

425 Sombart, 1906, p. 20.

426 As quoted in McCoy, 2012. For more on Lovestone, born Jacob Liebstein, see Morgan, 1999.

427 Rodgers as referred to in McCoy, 2012.

428 Myrdal, 1944.

429 The metaphor of the melting pot was popularized by the playwright Israel Zangwill's 1908 drama *The Melting Pot*.

430 Lipset, 1996, p. 19, 20, 22.

431 *Ibid*, p. 26.

432 *Ibid*, p. 268.

433 Conrad, 2014, p. 322.

434 Schuck and Wilson, 2008, p. 597, 598.

435 White House press release, April 4, 2009.

436 For critical comments on this kind of listing, see, for example, Smith, 1997.

437 Schlesinger, 1959.

438 For more on the origins of the US Constitution, see Kammen, 1986.

439 See, for example, Friedman, Lawrence, "The Legal System" in Schuck and Wilson, 2008.

440 Conrad, 2014, p. 327.

441 Stratfor, 2011(a), p. 10, 11.

442 Stratfor, 2011(b), p. 7.

443 de Tocqueville, 1835–40, p. 500–503.

444 *Ibid*.

445 Krauthammer in the *Washington Post*, April 19, 2012.

446 Krauthammer in the *Washington Post*, February 12, 2010.

447 Taken from "John F. Kennedy—1960 Democratic National Convention Address," *American Rhetoric*.

448 Forbes, 1968, p. 203.

449 The frontier culture even led to outright mythology as symbolized by the figure of Paul Bunyan. See Hoffman, 1999.

450 Turner, 1893. See also Turner, 1921. For a critique on Turner's view on the frontier issue, see Nelson Limerick, 1987.

451 Turner, 1893.

452 *Ibid*.

453 Benjamin Franklin, a Founding Father often referred to as "the first American," was a politician, a diplomat, a scientist, and an inventor. See Brands, 2000.

454 Bush, 1945, p. 4.

455 By the time Bush finalized his report, Franklin Roosevelt had died and had been succeeded by Harry Truman.

456 Bush, 1945, p. 2.

457 Schlesinger, 1959.

458 Wilson as quoted in Reynolds, 2009, p. 305.

459 Schuck in Schuck and Wilson, 2008, p. 321.

460 See, for example, Ewing, 2012.

461 See Wadhwa, 2012 and *The Economist*, 2014(a).

462 See for example, Rector, 2007 and Camarota, 2011.

463 See the evidence assembled in Fitz, Wolgin, and Oakford, 2013.

464 Roberston as quoted on November 28, 2011 on canadianreporter.worldpress.com.

465 *The Economist*, April 13, 2013, p. 55–56.

466 *Ibid.*, p. 56.

467 See Wadhwa, 2012 and Wadhwa et al., 2007.

468 Schuck in Schuck and Wilson, 2008, p. 349, 350.

469 Kagan, 2012, p. 132.

470 For more on political dysfunction in the United States, see, for example, Fukuyama, 2014 and Mann, 2014.

471 Dionne in the *Washington Post*, February 27, 2013.

472 Kazin in *The New Republic* online, March 7, 2011.

473 *Time*, November 12, 2012.

474 Thomas Heffner, 2014, "America's Flawed Political System," *Economy in Crisis*, October 19.

475 DeLong, 2012.

476 Robert Merry in *The National Interest*, May–June 2012.

477 Kagan, 2012, p. 131.

478 Nye, 2010, p. 9 and p. 5.

479 DeLong, 2012.

480 NCFRR, 2010, p. 7, 8. The National Commission on Fiscal Responsibility and Reform was a bipartisan group created by President Barack Obama and is often referred to as the Simpson–Bowles Commission after its two chairmen: retired senator Alan Simpson and former White House chief of staff Erskine Bowles. See National Commission on Fiscal Responsibility and Reform, 2010.

481 Kotlikoff on BloombergBusiness.com, August 11, 2010.

482 For a more exhaustive argumentation in this respect, see, for example, Mauldin and Tepper, 2011. For the history of America as a debtor nation, see Hyman, 2012. For an interesting link between debt dynamics and democracy, see MacDonald, 2006.

483 For more details on the debt increase, see, for example, the Pew Fiscal Analysis Initiative, 2011.

484 Data taken from Buttiglione et al., 2014. These data do not always fully correspond with those of, for example, the OECD.

485 It needs to be added here that state and local debt are not counted here as neither the enormous debt of the so-called government-sponsored enterprises such as Fannie Mae and Freddie Mac is. But also in other countries debt statistics do not count all of the government debt that is really floating around. This caveat certainly holds for emerging market countries. China is a prime example.

486 High government debt leads to crowding out of private investment, increases the risk of rising interest rates, and increases the risk of destabilizing central bank policies.

487 The American Society of Civil Engineers releases every four years its Report Card for America's Infrastructure that reports on the condition and performance of the nation's infrastructure. In its 2013 report, the investment needed to bring the American infrastructure again up-to-date by 2020 was estimated to be…$3.6 trillion.

488 To put the 9 percent of GDP figure of the US in perspective, the comparable figure for Brazil is 7 percent, for the UK 6 percent, for Canada 4 percent, for Germany 3 percent, and for Japan 1.5 percent.

489 Obama as quoted by the Associated Press, December 4, 2013.

490 Stiglitz, 2012, p. xlii.

491 Manzi, 2010.

492 Putnam as quoted in *Der Spiegel*, November 1, 2010.

493 Data taken from Brynjolfsson and McAfee, 2014, p. 133.

494 The following data are taken from Gordon, 2013.

495 See Frank and Cook, 1996; Brynjolfsson and McAfee, 2011; and Kaplan and Rauh, 2013. The seminal analysis of the economics of superstars remains Rosen, 1981.

496 For a more elaborate discussion on these issues, see Brynjolfsson and McAfee, 2014, especially Chapter 10.

497 For some strong statements in this respect, see Turner, 2014.

498 See, for example, OECD, 2011.

499 See Boudreaux and Perry, 2013 and Perry, 2013.

500 Auten, Gee, and Turner, 2013, p. 894.

501 *Ibid.,* p. 906.

502 Burtless, 2014.

503 *Ibid.*

504 The seminal work on overreach remains Kennedy, 1987.

505 See, for example, Reid, 2004; Rifkin, 2004; Leonard, 2005; and Hill, 2010. See also Thurow, 1992. For a powerful counter-argumentation, see, for example, Laqueur, 2007; Bongiovanni, 2012; Hewitt, 2013; and Soros, 2014. For the contrast between Europe and the United States, see Gregg, 2013.

506 Not all EU members stepped into the monetary union. At the moment of finalizing this book (January 2015) 18 of the 28 members of the EU are part of the euro area.

507 Laqueur, 2007, p. 15.

508 See Van Overtveldt, 2011 for more background.

509 As editor of the Flemish weekly *Trends*, I was among the few who pointed out from the beginning the institutional incompleteness of Europe's monetary union and who warned for the untenable tensions building up inside the euro area.

510 Most decisive in the turnaround was the promise Mario Draghi, president of the European Central Bank, made: "The ECB is ready to do whatever it takes to preserve the euro. And believe me, it will be enough." (Speech by Draghi at the Global Investment Conference in London, July 26, 2012.)

511 Alesina and Giavazzi, 2006, p. 165.

512 Subramanian, 2011.

513 Jacques, 2009, p. 20

514 Halper, 2010.

515 Miliband as quoted in *The Guardian*, May 17, 2009.

516 Parfitt, 2012.

517 Wen Jiabao as quoted in *The Guardian*, March 5, 2013.

518 Mao Yushi as quoted in the *Financial Times*, May 2, 2014.

519 *The Economist*, January 25, 2014, p. 7.

520 Beckley, 2011.

521 Fenby, 2014.

522 Pettis, 2013.

523 Kagan, 2012, p. 69.

524 Shambaugh, 2013, p. x.

525 Pei, 2010.

526 Li on YaleGlobal Online, November 19, 2013.

527 Chang, 2001, p. xvi, xviii.

528 French China-watcher Jean-Luc Domenach wrote a book (2008, Paris, Edition Perrin) entitled *La Chine m'Inquiète* ("China worries me").

529 Maddison, 2007, p. 15, 16, and 17. Maddison's analysis provides all the data used here to paint a picture of China's economic development. On China's institutional evolution over the centuries, see also Acemoglu and Robinson, 2012.

530 Maddison, 2007, p. 19.

531 The sheer madness of some of Mao's initiatives is illustrated by the fact that when some of the atrocities committed during the Cultural Revolution by his Red Guard were laid out before him, the Chairman retorted: "The more people you kill, the more revolutionary you are." Mao as quoted in Acemoglu and Robinson, 2012, p. 422.

532 Zhu, 2013, p. 103.

533 Books and analyses on China's economic rise are numerous. See, for example, Huang, 2008; Zhu, 2013; and Morrison, 2013.

534 Substantial doubts exist about the reliability of the Chinese growth data. There are serious indications that the authorities continuously manipulate the data to bring them in accordance with what is deemed necessary from a political point of view. On these issues, see, for example, Wu, 2006.

535 Musharraf on BBC News, November 5, 2003.

536 Kissinger, 2012, p. 546.

537 Data taken from Stephen Roach, 2014, "China's Monetary-Policy Surprise," *Project Syndicate*, November 22.

538 Green, 2014.

539 Basu in the *Financial Times*, April 27, 2014.

540 See, for example, Walter and Howie, 2011.

541 All these debt data are taken from the Bank for International Settlements.

542 Halper, 2010, p. 209.

543 Reinhart and Rogoff, 2009.

544 Actually, Irving Fisher (1867–1947), one of the most remarkable figures in the history of economic thought, labeled his theory "The Debt-Deflation Theory of Great Depressions." The correction of overindebtedness almost always sets in motion corrections that push economies into, or at least to the verge of, a depression. See Fisher, 1933.

545 See, for example, the discussion in the *Financial Times*, December 2, 2014.

546 In European countries like Ireland, Greece, and Italy, the debt to GDP ratios stand far above the 100 percent mark.

547 In early 2014, China planned 55 new airports at a moment that three quarters of existing airports were loosing money. Reported on CNBC.com, February 11, 2014.

548 *The Economist*, October 18, 2014.

549 As a matter of fact, deflationary pressures are already clearly discernable in the Chinese economy. The producer prices index, not to be confused with the consumer price index, is on a downward trend since the second half of 2011.

550 See, for example, the reporting in "Distressed Debt in China? Ain't Seen Nothing, DAC Says," Bloomberg, November 20, 2014 and "China's Banks Are Getting Ready for a Debt Implosion," *Business Insider*, October 16, 2014.

551 Jin, 2014. On the structural problems of China's growth model, see also, for example, Hoffman and Polk, 2014.

552 Krugman in the *New York Times*, July 18, 2013.

553 Li as quoted in the *Financial Times*, March 19, 2014.

554 See, for example, the data provided in Hoffman and Polk, 2014.

555 Jin, 2014.

556 The Chinese authorities are well aware of this major problem. See, for example, the reporting by Stratfor Global Intelligence, 2013, "In China, an Unprecedented Demographic Problem Takes Shape," August 21.

557 OECD Observer, No. 217-218, summer 1999.

558 *The Economist*, April 21, 2012.

559 *Financial Times*, November 6, 2013.

560 Data quoted in *The National Interest*, September 25, 2014.

561 See Tiezzi, 2013.

562 The data in this paragraph are taken from Pew Research, 2014, Chapter 2. For more on American demographics, see Kotkin, 2010.

563 Among the major countries in the world, the increase in the median age is worst in Asia and in Europe. In South Korea the median age jumps from 38 to 53, in Japan from 45 to 53, in Germany from 44 to 51, in Spain from 40 to 50, and in Italy from 43 to 50.

564 See, for example, the reporting in *The Atlantic*, April 18, 2014. The Huffington Post carries a special section on China pollution.

565 Exxon Mobil, 2009, "The Outlook for Energy: A View to 2030."

566 As reported in the *New York Times*, February 20, 2013.

567 Hsu, 2013.

568 See, for example, the data on numbeo.com. For a comparison between the two countries with respect to air pollution, see the contribution of Bill Chameides, dean of Duke University's Nicholas School of the Environment, on Huffingtonpost.com, April 2, 2014.

569 For some data on the cost of corruption, see, for example, Mei, 2007.

570 Lu, 2000.

571 Xuecun, 2012.

572 Xi as quoted on Bloomberg.com, March 4, 2014.

573 Nanayakkara, 2014.

574 Hoffman and Polk, 2014, p. 12.

575 As reported in the *New York Times*, October 12, 2012.

576 New GFI Report, October 25, 2012.

577 See Hoffman and Polk, 2014 for more details.

578 As reported on Bloomberg.com, April 29, 2014.

579 *Ibid.*

580 See, for example, several polls conducted by Pew Research.

581 Data available on Chinaoutlook.com. More recent data on the absolute number of mass incidents in China do not seem to be available.

582 Young-Kwan on Project Syndicate: "The Asian Paradox," November 4, 2014.

583 Kagan, 2012, p. 69. On the intra-Asian power relationships and their international ramifications, see Emmott, 2008.

584 Point stressed in, for example, Cox, 2011.

585 Hu Jintao as quoted in Nathan and Gilley, 2003, p. 206.

586 *The Economist*, October 4, 2014, p. 13.

587 Zhang Jun, professor of economics and director of the China Center for Economic Studies at Fudan University in Shanghai, fundamentally dissents with this view. See Jun, 2014.

588 Miller as quoted in *The Guardian*, December 23, 2013. See also, for example, Klare, 2004 for some apocalyptic insights on what an oil shortage might bring about.

589 *Titusville Herald*, July 19, 1909.

590 *Christian Science Monitor*, September 18, 1918.

591 *Brooklyn Daily Eagle*, March 9, 1937.

592 *Corpus Christi Times*, March 9, 1957. Hubbert proved to be relatively well on the mark in terms of the production of conventional oil in the United States.

593 Data taken from the *BP Statistical Review of World Energy*, June 2014.

594 Deutch, 2011, p. 82.

595 IEA online press release, "Supply Shock from North American Oil Rippling Through Global Markets," May 14, 2013.

596 This question was the cover title of *The Atlantic*, April 24, 2013.

597 For more on the shale revolution and its characteristics and many consequences, see, for example, Hastings Dunn and McClelland, 2013; Maugeri, 2013; and Morris, 2013. Zuckerman, 2013 tells the fascinating story of the many entrepreneurial pioneers who created the shale revolution.

598 For more on this reindustrialization process, see, for example, the report prepared by Euler Hermes, the largest credit insurer of the world (*The Re-industrialization of the USA*, December 2012, updated April, 2014). See also the analysis prepared by the Boston Consulting Group (*Made in America, Again*, August 2011).

599 See, for example, Yergin, 2014.

600 West as quoted in Hastings Dunn and McClelland, 2013, p. 1428.

601 Hastings Dunn and McClelland, 2013, p. 1412.

602 *The Economist,* December 6, 2014.

603 Verleger in an interview on National Public Radio on March 7, 2012 (taken from Carpe Diem, professor Mark J. Perry's Blog for Economics and Finance).

604 *The Economist,* February 15, 2014.

605 Yergin, Daniel, "There Will Be Oil," *Wall Street Journal,* September 27, 2011.

606 Mills in the *Wall Street Journal,* October 23, 2014.

607 As most of the time this discussion is complex. While, for example, fracking entails undeniable ecological costs, the substitution of coal by natural gas brings major ecological benefits.

608 Churchill as quoted in Kagan, 2012, p. 15.

Index